George Rawlinson

The History of Babylon

e-artnow 2018

George Rawlinson
The History of Babylon

e-artnow, 2018
Contact: info@e-artnow.org

ISBN 978-80-273-3177-2

Contents

Chapter I. Extent of the Empire	11
Chapter II. Climate and Productions	29
Chapter III. The People	37
Chapter IV. The Capital	45
Chapter V. Arts and Sciences	61
Chapter VI. Manners and Customs	83
Chapter VII. Religion	99
Chapter VIII. History and Chronology	103
Appendix.	121

Chapter I. Extent of the Empire

"Behold, a tree in the midst of the earth, and the height thereof was great; the tree grew and was strong: and the height thereof reached unto heaven, and the sight thereof to the end of all the earth." —Dan. iy. 10, 11.

The limits of Babylonia Proper, the tract in which the dominant power of the Fourth Monarchy had its abode, being almost identical with those which have been already described under the head of Chaldaea, will not require in this place to be treated afresh, at any length. It needs only to remind the reader that Babylonia Proper is that alluvial tract towards the mouth of the two great rivers of Western Asia-the Tigris and the Euphrates-which intervenes between the Arabian Desert on the one side, and the more eastern of the two streams on the other. Across the Tigris the country is no longer Babylonia, but Cissia, or Susiana —a distinct region, known to the Jews as Elam-the habitat of a distinct people. Babylonia lies westward of the Tigris, and consists of two vast plains or flats, one situated between the two rivers, and thus forming the lower portion of the "Mesopotamia" of the Greeks and Romans-the other interposed between the Euphrates and Arabia, a long but narrow strip along the right bank of that abounding river. The former of these two districts is shaped like an ancient amphora, the mouth extending from Hit to Samarah, the neck lying between Baghdad and Ctesiphon on the Tigris, Mohammed and Mosaib on the Euphrates, the full expansion of the body occurring between Serut and El Khithr, and the pointed base reaching down to Kornah at the junction of the two streams. This tract, the main region of the ancient Babylonia, is about 320 miles long, and from 20 to 100 broad. It may be estimated to contain about 18,000 square miles. The tract west of the Euphrates is smaller than this. Its length, in the time of the Babylonian Empire, may be regarded as about 350 miles, its average width is from 25 to 30 miles, which would give an area of about 9000 square miles. Thus the Babylonia of Nabopolassar and Nebuchadnezzar may be regarded as covering a space of 27,000 square miles —a space a little exceeding the area of the Low countries.

The small province included within these limits-smaller than Scotland or Ireland, or Portugal or Bavaria-became suddenly, in the latter half of the seventh century B.C., the mistress of an extensive empire. On the fall of Assyria, about B.C. 625, or a little later, Media and Babylonia, as already observed, divided between them her extensive territory. It is with the acquisitions thus made that we have now to deal. We have to inquire what portion exactly of the previous dominions of Assyria fell to the lot of the adventurous Nabopolassar, when Nineveh ceased to be-what was the extent of the territory which was ruled from Babylon in the latter portion of the seventh and the earlier portion of the sixth century before our era?

Now the evidence which we possess on this point is threefold. It consists of certain notices in the Hebrew Scriptures, contemporary records of first-rate historical value; of an account which strangely mingles truth with fable in one of the books of the Apocrypha; and of a passage of Berosus preserved by Josephus in his work against Apion. The Scriptural notices are contained in Jeremiah, in Daniel, and in the books of Kings and Chronicles. From these sources we learn that the Babylonian Empire of this time embraced on the one hand the important country of Susiana or Elymais (Elam), while on the other it ran up the Euphrates at least as high as Carchemish, from thence extending westward to the Mediterranean, and southward to, or rather perhaps into, Egypt. The Apocryphal book of Judith enlarges these limits in every direction. That the Nabuchodonosor of that work is a reminiscence of the real Nebuchadnezzar there can be no doubt. The territories of that monarch are made to extend eastward, beyond Susiana, into Persia; northward to Nineveh; westward to Cilicia in Asia Minor; and southward to the very borders of Ethiopia. Among the countries under his sway are enumerated Elam, Persia, Assyria, Cilicia, Coele-Syria, Syria of Damascus, Phoenicia, Galilee, Gilead, Bashan, Judsea,

Philistia, Goshen, and Egypt generally. The passage of Berosus is of a more partial character. It has no bearing on the general question of the extent of the Babylonian Empire, but, incidentally, it confirms the statements of our other authorities as to the influence of Babylon in the West. It tells us that Coele-Syria, Phoenicia, and Egypt, were subject to Nabopolassar, and that Nebuchadnezzar ruled, not only over these countries, but also over some portion of Arabia.

From these statements, which, on the whole, are tolerably accordant, we may gather that the great Babylonian Empire of the seventh century B.C. inherited from Assyria all the southern and western portion of her territory, while the more northern and eastern provinces fell to the share of Media. Setting aside the statement of the book of Judith (wholly unconfirmed as it is by any other authority), that Persia was at this time subject to Babylon, we may regard as the most eastern portion of the Empire the district of Susiana, which corresponded nearly with the modern Khuzistan and Luristan. This acquisition advanced the eastern frontier of the Empire from the Tigris to the Bakhtiyari Mountains, a distance of 100 or 120 miles. It gave to Babylon an extensive tract of very productive territory, and an excellent strategic boundary. Khuzistan is one of the most valuable provinces of modern Persia. It consists of a broad tract of fertile alluvium, intervening between the Tigris and the mountains, well watered by numerous large streams, which are capable of giving an abundant irrigation to the whole of the low region. Above this is Luristan, a still more pleasant district, composed of alternate mountain, valley, and upland plain, abounding in beautiful glens, richly wooded, and full of gushing brooks and clear rapid rivers. Much of this region is of course uncultivable mountain, range succeeding range, in six or eight parallel lines, as the traveller advances to the north-east; and most of the ranges exhibiting vast tracts of bare and often precipitous rock, in the clefts of which snow rests till midsummer. Still the lower flanks of the mountains are in general cultivable, while the valleys teem with orchards and gardens, and the plains furnish excellent pasture. The region closely resembles Zagros, of which it is a continuation. As we follow it, however, towards the south-east into the Bakhtiyari country, where it adjoins upon the ancient Persia, it deteriorates in character; the mountains becoming barer and more arid, and the valleys narrower and less fertile.

All the other acquisitions of Babylonia at this period lay towards the west. They consisted of the Euphrates valley, above Hit; of Mesopotamia Proper, or the country about the two streams of the Bilik and the Khabour; of Syria, Phoenicia, Palestine, Idumasa, Northern Arabia, and part of Egypt. The Euphrates valley from Hit to Balis is a tract of no great value, except as a line of communication. The Mesopotamian Desert presses it closely upon the one side, and the Arabian upon the other. The river flows mostly in a deep bed between cliffs of marl, gypsum, and limestone, or else between bare hills producing only a few dry sapless shrubs and a coarse grass; and there are but rare places where, except by great efforts, the water can be raised so as to irrigate, to any extent, the land along either bank. The course of the stream is fringed by date-palms as high as Anah, and above is dotted occasionally with willows, poplars, sumacs, and the unfruitful palm-tree. Cultivation is possible in places along both banks, and the undulating country on either side affords patches of good pasture. The land improves as we ascend. Above the junction of the Khabour with the main stream, the left bank is mostly cultivable. Much of the land is flat and well-wooded, while often there are broad stretches of open ground, well adapted for pasturage. A considerable population seems in ancient times to have peopled the valley, which did not depend wholly or even mainly on its own products, but was enriched by the important traffic which was always passing up and down the great river.

Mesopotamia Proper, or the tract extending from the head streams of the Khabour about Mardin and Nisibin to the Euphrates at Bir, and thence southwards to Karkesiyeh or Circesium, is not certainly known to have belonged to the kingdom of Babylon, but may be assigned to it on grounds of probability. Divided by a desert or by high mountains from the valley of the Tigris, and attached by means of its streams to that of the Euphrates, it almost necessarily falls to that power which holds the Euphrates under its dominion. The tract is one of considerable extent and importance. Bounded on the north by the range of hills which Strabo calls Mons Masius, and on the east by the waterless upland which lies directly west of the middle Tigris, it comprises within it all the numerous affluents of the Khabour and Bilik, and is thus better supplied with water than almost any country in these regions. The borders of the streams afford the richest pasture, and the whole tract along the flank of Masius is fairly fertile. Towards the west, the tract between the Khabour and the Bilik, which is diversified by the Abd-el-Aziz hills, is a land of fountains. "Such," says Ibn Haukal, "are not to be found elsewhere in all the land of the Moslems, for there are more than three hundred pure running brooks." Irrigation is quite possible in this region; and many remains of ancient watercourses show that large tracts, at some distance from the main streams, were formerly brought under cultivation.

Opposite to Mesopotamia Proper, on the west or right bank of the Euphrates, lay Northern Syria, with its important fortress of Carchemish, which was undoubtedly included in the Empire. This tract is not one of much value. Towards the north it is mountainous, consisting of spurs from Amanus and Taurus, which gradually subside into the desert a little to the south of Aleppo. The bare, round-backed, chalky or rocky ranges, which here continually succeed one another, are divided only by narrow tortuous valleys, which run chiefly towards the Euphrates or the lake of Antioch. This mountain tract is succeeded by a region of extensive plains, separated from each other by low hills, both equally desolate. The soil is shallow and stony; the streams are few and of little volume; irrigation is thus difficult, and, except where it can be applied, the crops are scanty. The pistachio-nut grows wild in places; Vines and olives are cultivated with some success; and some grain is raised by the inhabitants; but the country has few natural advantages, and it has always depended more upon its possession of a carrying trade than on its home products for prosperity.

West and south-west of this region, between it and the Mediterranean, and extending southwards from Mount Amanus to the latitude of Tyre, lies Syria Proper, the Coele-Syria of many writers, a long but comparatively narrow tract of great fertility and value. Here two parallel ranges of mountains intervene between the coast and the desert, prolific parents of a numerous progeny of small streams. First, along the line of the coast, is the range known as Libanus in the south, from lat. 33° 20' to lat. 34° 40', and as Bargylus in the north, from lat. 34° 45' to the Orontes at Antioch, a range of great beauty, richly wooded in places, and abounding in deep glens, foaming brooks, and precipices of a fantastic form. More inland is Antilibanus, culminating towards the south in Hermon, and prolonged northward in the Jebel Shashabu, Jebel Biha, and Jebel-el-Ala, which extends from near Hems to the latitude of Aleppo. More striking than even Lebanon at its lower extremity, where Hermon lifts a snowy peak into the air during most of the year, it is on the whole inferior in beauty to the coast range, being bleaker, more stony, and less broken up by dells and valleys towards the south, and tamer, barer, and less well supplied with streams in its more northern portion. Between the two parallel ranges lies the "Hollow Syria," a long and broadish valley, watered by the two streams of the Orontes and the "Litany" which, rising at no great distance from one another, flow in opposite directions, one hurrying northwards nearly to the flanks of Amanus, the other southwards to the hills of Galilee. Few places in the world are more, remarkable, or have a more stirring history, than this wonderful vale. Extending for above two hundred miles from north to south, almost in a direct line, and without further break than an occasional screen of low hills, it furnishes the most convenient line of passage between Asia and Africa, alike for the journeys of merchants and for the march of armies. Along this line passed Thothines and Barneses, Sargon, and Sennacherib, Neco and Nebuchadnezzar, Alexander and his warlike successors, Pompey, Antony, Kaled, Godfrey of Bouillon; along this must pass every great army which, starting from the general seats of power in Western Asia, seeks conquests in Africa, or which, proceeding from Africa, aims at the acquisition of an Asiatic dominion. Few richer tracts are to be found even in these most favored portions of the earth's surface. Towards the south the famous El-Bukaa is a land of cornfields and vineyards, watered by numerous small streams which fall into the Litany. Towards the north El-Ghab is even more splendidly fertile, with a dark rich soil, luxuriant vegetation, and water in the utmost abundance, though at present it is cultivated only in patches immediately about the towns, from fear of the Nusairiyeh and the Bedouins.

View of the Lebanon range.

Parallel with the southern part of the Coele-Syrian valley, to the west and to the east, were two small but important tracts, usually regarded as distinct states. Westward, between the heights of Lebanon and the sea, and extending somewhat beyond Lebanon, both up and down the coast, was Phoenicia, a narrow strip of territory lying along the shore, in length from 150 to 180 miles, and in breadth varying from one mile to twenty. This tract consisted of a mere belt of sandy land along the sea, where the smiling palm-groves grew from which the country derived its name, of a broader upland region along the flank of the hills, which was cultivated in grain, and of the higher slopes of the mountains which furnished excellent timber. Small harbors, sheltered by rocky projections, were frequent along the coast. Wood cut in Lebanon was readily floated down the many streams to the shore, and then conveyed by sea to the ports. A narrow and scanty land made commerce almost a necessity. Here accordingly the first great maritime nation of antiquity grew up. The Phoenician fleets explored the Mediterranean at a time anterior to Homer, and conveyed to the Greeks and the other inhabitants of Europe, and of Northern and Western Africa, the wares of Assyria, Babylon, and Egypt. Industry and enterprise reaped their usual harvest of success; the Phoenicians grew in wealth, and their towns became great and magnificent cities. In the time when the Babylonian Empire came into being, the narrow tract of Phoenicia-smaller than many an English county-was among the most valuable countries of Asia; and its possession was far more to be coveted than that of many a land whose area was ten or twenty times as great.

Eastward of Antilibanus, in the tract between that range and the great Syrian desert, was another very important district-the district which the Jews called "Aram-Dammesek," and which now forms the chief part of the Pashalik of Damascus. From the eastern flanks of the Antilibanus two great and numerous smaller streams flow down into the Damascene plain, and, carrying with them that strange fertilizing power which water always has in hot climates, convert the arid sterility of the desert into a garden of the most wonderful beauty. The Barada and Awaaj, bursting by narrow gorges from the mountain chain, scatter themselves in numerous channels over the great flat, intermingling their waters, and spreading them out so widely that for a circle of thirty miles the deep verdure of Oriental vegetation replaces the red hue of the Hauran. Walnuts, planes, poplars, cypresses, apricots, orange-trees, citrons, pomegranates, olives, wave above; corn and grass of the most luxuriant growth, below. In the midst of this great mass of foliage the city of Damascus "strikes out the white arms of its streets hither and thither" among the trees, now hid among them, now overtopping them with its domes and minarets, the most beautiful of all those beautiful towns which delight the eye of the artist in the East. In the south-west towers the snow-clad peak of Hermon, visible from every part of the Damascene plain. West, north-west, and north, stretches the long Antilibanus range, bare, gray, and flat-topped, except where about midway in its course, the rounded summit of Jebel Tiniyen breaks the uniformity of the line. Outside the circle of deep verdure, known to the Orientals as El Merj ("the Meadow"), is a setting or framework of partially cultivable land, dotted with clumps of trees and groves, which extend for many miles over the plain. To the Damascus country must also be reckoned those many charming valleys of Hermon and Antilibanus which open out into it, sending their waters to increase its beauty and luxuriance, the most remarkable of which are the long ravine of the Barada, and the romantic Wady Halbon, whose vines produced the famous beverage which Damascus anciently supplied at once to the Tyrian merchant-princes and to the voluptuous Persian kings.

Below the Coelo-Syrian valley, towards the south, came Palestine, the Land of Lands to the Christian, the country which even the philosopher must acknowledge to have had a greater influence on the world's history than any other tract which can be brought under a single ethnic designation. Palestine-etymologically the country of the Philistines-was somewhat unfortunately named. Philistine influence may possibly have extended at a very remote period over the whole of it; but in historical times that warlike people did but possess a corner of the tract, less than one tenth of the whole-the low coast region from Jamnia to Gaza. Palestine contained, besides this, the regions of Galilee, Samaria, and Judaea, to the west of the Jordan, and those of Ituraea, Trachonitis, Bashan, and Gilead, east of that river. It was a tract 140 miles long, by from 70 to 100 broad, containing probably about 11,000 square miles. It was thus about equal in size to Belgium, while it was less than Holland or Hanover, and not much larger than the principality of Wales, with which it has been compared by a recent writer.

The great natural division of the country is the Jordan valley. This remarkable depression, commencing on the west flank of Hermon, runs with a course which is almost due south from lat. 33° 25' to lat. 31° 47', where it is merged in the Dead Sea, which may be viewed, however, as a continuation of the valley, prolonging it to lat. 31° 8'. This valley is quite unlike any other in the whole world. It is a volcanic rent in the earth's surface, a broad chasm which has gaped and never closed up. Naturally, it should terminate at Merom, where the level of the Mediterranean is nearly reached. By some wonderful convulsion, or at any rate by some unusual freak of Nature, there is a channel opened out from Merom, which rapidly sinks below the sea level, and allows the stream to flow hastily, down and still down, from Merom to Gennesareth, and from Gennesareth to the Dead Sea, where the depression reaches its lowest point, and the land, rising into a ridge, separates the Jordan valley from the upper end of the Gulf of Akabah. The Jordan valley divides Palestine, strongly and sharply, into two regions. Its depth, its inaccessibility (for it can only be entered from the highlands on either side down a few steep watercourses), and the difficulty of passing across it (for the Jordan has but few fords), give it a separating power almost equal to that of an arm of the sea. In length above a hundred miles, in width varying from one mile to ten, and averaging some five miles, or perhaps six, it must have been valuable as a territory, possessing, as it does, a rich soil, abundant water, and in its lower portion a tropical climate.

On either side of the deep Jordan cleft lies a highland of moderate elevation, on the right that of Galilee, Samaria, and Judsea, on the left that of Ituraea, Bashan, and Gilead. The right or western highland consists of a mass of undulating hills, with rounded tops, composed of coarse gray stone, covered, or scarcely covered, with a scanty soil, but capable of cultivation in corn, olives, and figs. This region is most productive towards the north, barer and more arid as we proceed southwards towards the desert. The lowest portion, Judaea, is unpicturesque, ill-watered, and almost treeless; the central, Samaria, has numerous springs, some rich plains, many wooded heights, and in places quite a sylvan appearance; the highest, Galilee, is a land of water-brooks, abounding in timber, fertile and beautiful. The average height of the whole district is from 1500 to 1800 feet above the Mediterranean. Main elevations within it vary from 2500 to 4000 feet. The axis of the range is towards the East, nearer, that is, to the Jordan valley than to the sea. It is a peculiarity of the highland that there is one important break in it. As the Lowland mountains of Scotland are wholly separated from the mountains of the Highlands by the low tract which stretches across from the Frith of Forth to the Frith of Clyde, or as the ranges of St. Gall and Appenzell are divided off from the rest of the Swiss mountains by the flat which extends from the Rhine at Eagatz to the same river at Waldshut, so the western highland of Palestine is broken in twain by the famous "plain of Esdraelon," which runs from the Bay of Acre to the Jordan valley at Beth-Shean or Scythopolis.

East of the Jordan no such depression occurs, the highland there being continuous. It differs from the western highland chiefly in this-that its surface, instead of being broken up into a confused mass of rounded hills, is a table-land, consisting of a long succession of slightly undulating plains. Except in Trachonitis and southern Ituraea, where the basaltic rock everywhere crops out, the soil is rich and productive, the country in places wooded with fine trees, and the herbage luxuriant. On the west the mountains rise almost precipitously from the Jordan valley, above which they tower to the height of 3000 or 4000 feet. The outline is singularly uniform; and the effect is that of a huge wall guarding Palestine on this side from the wild tribes of the desert. Eastward the tableland slopes gradually, and melts into the sands of Arabia. Here water and wood are scarce; but the soil is still good, and bears the most abundant crops.

Finally, Palestine contains the tract from which it derives its name, the low country of the Philistines, which the Jews called the *Shephelah*, together with a continuation of this tract northwards to the roots of Carmol, the district known to the Jews as "Sharon," or "the smooth place." From Carmol to the Wady Sheriah, where the Philistine country ended, is a distance of about one hundred miles, which gives the length of the region in question. Its breadth between the shore and the highland varies from about twenty-five miles, in the south, between Gaza and the hills of Dan, to three miles, or less, in the north, between Dor and the border of Manasseh. Its area is probably from 1400 to 1500 square miles, This low strip is along its whole course divided into two parallel belts or bands-the first a flat sandy tract along the shore, the Ramleh of the modern Arabs; the second, more undulating, a region of broad rolling plains rich in corn, and anciently clothed in part with thick woods, watered by reedy streams, which flow down from the great highland. A valuable tract is this entire plain, but greatly exposed to ravage. Even the sandy belt will grow fruit-trees; and the towns which stand on it, as Gaza, Jaffa, and Ashdod, are surrounded with huge groves of olives, sycamores, and palms, or buried in orchards and gardens, bright with pomegranates and orange-trees. The more inland region is of marvellous fertility. Its soil is a rich loam, containing scarcely a pebble, which yields year after year prodigious crops of grain-chiefly wheat-without manure or irrigation, or other cultivation than a light ploughing. Philistia was the granary of Syria, and was important doubly, first, as yielding inexhaustible supplies to its conqueror, and secondly as affording the readiest passage to the great armies which contended in these regions for the mastery of the Eastern World.

South of the region to which we have given the name of Palestine, intervening between it and Egypt, lay a tract, to which it is difficult to assign any political designation. Herodotus regarded it as a portion of Arabia, which he carried across the valley of the Arabah and made abut on the Mediterranean. To the Jews it was "the land of the south" —the special country of the Amalekites. By Strabo's time it had come to be known as Idumsea, or the Edomite country; and under this appellation it will perhaps be most convenient to describe it here. Idumasa, then, was the tract south and south-west of Palestine from about lat. 31° 10'. It reached westward to the borders of Egypt, which were at this time marked by the Wady-el-Arish, southward to the range of Sinai and the Elanitic Gulf, and eastward to the Great Desert. Its chief town was Petra, in the mountains east of the Arabah valley. The character of the tract is for the most part a hard gravelly and rocky desert; but occasionally there is good herbage, and soil that admits of cultivation; brilliant flowers and luxuriantly growing shrubs bedeck the glens and terraces of the Petra range; and most of the tract produces plants and bushes on which camels, goats, and even sheep will browse, while occasional palm groves furnish a grateful shade and an important fruit. The tract divides itself into four regions-first, a region of sand, low and flat, along the Mediterranean, the Shephelah without its fertility; next, a region of hard gravelly plain intersected by limestone ridges, and raised considerably above the sea level, the Desert of El-Tin, or of "the Wanderings;" then the long, broad, low valley of the Arabah, which rises gradually from the Dead Sea to an imperceptible watershed, and then falls gently to the head of the Gulf of Akabah, a region of hard sand thickly dotted with bushes, and intersected by numerous torrent courses; finally a long narrow region of mountains and hills parallel with the Arabah, constituting Idumsea Proper, or the original Edom, which, though rocky and rugged, is full of fertile glens, ornamented with trees and shrubs, and in places cultivated in terraces. In shape the tract was a rude square or oblong, with its sides nearly facing the four cardinal points, its length from the Mediterranean to the Gulf of Akabah being 130 miles, and its width from the Wady-el-Arish to the eastern side of the Petra mountains 120 miles. The area is thus about 1560 square miles.

Beyond the Wady-el-Arish was Egypt, stretching from the Mediterranean southwards a distance of nearly eight degrees, or more than 550 miles. As this country was not, however, so much a part of the Babylonian Empire as a dependency lying upon its borders, it will not be necessary to describe it in this place.

One region, however, remains still unnoticed which seems to have been an integral portion of the Empire. This is Palmyrene, or the Syrian Desert-the tract lying between Coelo-Syria on the one hand and the valley of the middle Euphrates on the other, and abutting towards the south on the great Arabian Desert, to which it is sometimes regarded as belonging. It is for the most part a hard sandy or gravelly plain, intersected by low rocky ranges, and either barren or productive only of some sapless shrubs and of a low thin grass. Occasionally, however, there are oases, where the fertility is considerable. Such an oasis is the region about Palmyra itself, which derived its name from the palm groves in the vicinity; here the soil is good, and a large tract is even now under cultivation. Another oasis is that of Karyatein, which is watered by an abundant stream, and is well wooded, and productive of grain. The Palmyrene, however, as a whole possesses but little value, except as a passage country. Though large armies can never have traversed the desert even in this upper region, where it is comparatively narrow, trade in ancient times found it expedient to avoid the long detour by the Orontes Valley, Aleppo, and Bambuk, and to proceed directly from Damascus by way of Palymra to Thapsaeus on the Euphrates. Small bands of light troops also occasionally took the same course; and the great saving of distance thus effected made it important to the Babylonians to possess an authority over the region in question.

Such, then, in its geographical extent, was the great Babylonian Empire. Reaching from Luristan on the one side to the borders of Egypt on the other, its direct length from east to west was nearly sixteen degrees, or about 980 miles, while its length for all practical purposes, owing to the interposition of the desert between its western and its eastern provinces, was perhaps not less than 1400 miles. Its width was very disproportionate to this. Between Zagros and the Arabian Desert, where the width was the greatest, it amounted to about 280 miles; between Amanus and Palmyra it was 250; between the Mons Masius and the middle Euphrates it may have been 200; in Syria and Idumsea it cannot have been more than 100 or 160. The entire area of the Empire was probably from 240,000 to 250,000 square miles-which is about the present size of Austria. Its shape may be compared roughly to a gnomon, with one longer and one shorter arm.

It added to the inconvenience of this long straggling form, which made a rapid concentration of the forces of the Empire impossible, that the capital, instead of occupying a central position, was placed somewhat low in the longer of the two arms of the gnomon, and was thus nearly 1000 miles removed from the frontier province of the west. Though in direct distance, as the crow flies, Babylon is not more than 450 miles from Damascus, or more than 520 from Jerusalem, yet the necessary detour by Aleppo is so great that it lengthens the distance, in the one case by 250, in the other by 380 miles. From so remote a centre it was impossible for the life-blood to circulate very vigorously to the extremities.

The Empire was on the whole fertile and well-watered. The two great streams of Western Asia-the Tigris and the Euphrates-which afforded an abundant supply of the invaluable fluid to the most important of the provinces, those of the south-east, have already been described at length; as have also the chief streams of the Mesopotamian district, the Belik and the Khabour. But as yet in this work no account has been given of a number of important rivers in the extreme east and the extreme west, on which the fertility, and so the prosperity, of the Empire very greatly depended. It is proposed in the present place to supply this deficiency.

The principle rivers of the extreme east were the Choaspes, or modern Kerkhah, the Pasitigris or Eulseus, now the Kuran, the Hedyphon or Hedypnus, now the Jerahi, and the Oroatis, at present the Tab or Hindyan. Of these, the Oroatis, which is the most eastern, belongs perhaps more to Persia than to Babylon; but its lower course probably fell within the Susianian territory. It rises in the mountains between Shiraz and Persepolis, about lat. 29° 45', long. 52° 35' E.; and flows towards the Persian Gulf with a course which is north-west to Failiyun, then nearly W. to Zehitun, after which it becomes somewhat south of west to Hindyan, and then S.W. by S. to the sea. The length of the stream, without counting lesser windings, is 200 miles; its width at Hindyan, sixteen miles above its mouth, is eighty yards, and to this distance it is navigable for boats of twenty tons burthen. At first its waters are pure and sweet, but they gradually become corrupted, and at Hindyan they are so brackish as not to be fit for use. The Jerahi rises from several sources in the Kuh Margun, a lofty and precipitous range, forming the continuation of the chain of Zagros. about long. 50° to 51°, and lat. 31° 30'. These head-streams have a general direction from N.E. to S.W. The principal of them is the Kurdistan river, which rises about fifty miles to the north-east of Babahan and flowing south-west to that point, then bends round to the north, and runs north-west nearly to the fort of Mungasht, where it resumes its original direction, and receiving from the north-east the Abi Zard, or "Yellow River" —a delightful stream of the coldest and purest water possible-becomes known as the Jerahi, and carries a large body of water as far as Fellahiyeh or Dorak. Near Dorak the waters of the Jerahi are drawn off into a number of canals, and the river is thus greatly diminished; but still the stream struggles on, and proceeds by a southerly course towards the Persian Gulf, which it enters near Gadi in long. 48° 52'. The course of the Jerahi, exclusively of the smaller windings, is about equal in length to that of the Tab or Hindyan. In volume, before its dispersion, it is considerably greater than that river. It has a breadth of about a hundred yards before it reaches Babahan, and is navigable for boats almost from its junction with the Abi Zard. Its size is, however, greatly reduced in its lower course, and travellers who skirt the coast regard the Tab as the more important river.

The Kuran is a river very much exceeding in size both the Tab and the Jerahi. It is formed by the junction of two large streams-the Dizful river and the Kuran proper, or river of Shuster. Of these the Shuster stream is the more eastern. It rises in the Zarduh Kuh, or "Yellow Mountain," in lat. 32°, long. 51°, almost opposite to the river Isfahan. From its source it is a large stream. Its direction is at first to the southeast, but after a while it sweeps round and runs considerably north of west; and this course it pursues through the mountains, receiving tributaries of importance from both sides, till, near Akhili, it turns round to the south, and, cutting at a right angle the outermost of the Zagros ranges, flows down with a course S.W. by S. nearly to Sinister, where, in consequence of a bund or dam thrown across it, it bifurcates, and passes in two streams to the right and to the left of the town. The right branch, which earned commonly about two thirds of the water, proceeds by a tortuous course of nearly forty miles, in a direction a very little west of south, to its junction with the Dizful stream, which takes place about two miles north of the little town of Bandi-kir. Just below that town the left branch, called at present Abi-Gargar, which has made a considerable bend to the east, rejoins the main stream, which thenceforth flows in a single channel. The course of the Kuran from its source to its junction with the Dizful branch, including main windings, is about 210 miles. The Dizful. branch rises from two sources, nearly a degree apart, in lat. 33° 30'. These streams run respectively south-east and south-west, a distance of forty miles, to their junction near Bahrein, whence their united waters flow in a tortuous course, with a general direction of south, for above a hundred miles to the outer barrier of Zagros, which they penetrate near the Diz fort, through a succession of chasms and gorges. The course of the stream from this point is south-west through the hills and across the plain, past Dizful, to the place where it receives the Beladrud from the west, when it changes and becomes first south and then southeast to its junction with the Shuster river near Bandi-kir. The entire course of the Dizful stream to this point is probably not less than 380 miles. Below Bandi-kir, the Kuran, now become "a noble river, exceeding in size the Tigris and Euphrates," meanders across the plain in a general direction of S.S. W., past the towns of Uris, Ahwaz, and Ismaili, to Sablah, when it turns more to the west, and passing Mohammerah, empties itself into the Shat-el-Arab, about 22 miles below Busra. The entire course of the Kuran from its most remote source, exclusive of the lesser windings, is not less than 430 miles.

The Kerkhah (anciently the Choaspes) is formed by three streams of almost equal magnitude, all of them rising in the most eastern portion of the Zagros range. The central of the three flows from the southern flank of Mount Elwand (Orontes), the mountain behind Hamadan (Ecbatana), and receives on the right, after a course of about thirty miles, the northern or Singur branch, and ten miles further on the southern or Guran branch, which is known by the name of the Gamas-ab. The river thus formed flows westward to Behistun, after which it bonds to the south-west, and then to the south, receiving tributaries on both hands, and winding among the mountains as far as the ruined city of Rudbar. Here it bursts through the outer barrier of the great range, and, receiving the large stream of the Kirrind from the north-west, flows S.S.E. and S.E. along the foot of the range, between it and the Kebir Kuh, till it meets the stream of the Abi-Zal, when it finally leaves the hills and flows through the plain, pursuing a S.S.E. direction to the ruins of Susa, which lie upon its left bank, and then turning to the S. S. W., and running in that direction to the Shat-el-Arab, which it reaches about five miles below Kurnur. Its length is estimated at above 500 miles; its width, at some distance above its junction with the Abi-Zal, is from eighty to a hundred yards.

The course of the Kerkhah was not always exactly such as is here described. Anciently it appears to have bifurcated at Pai Pul, 18 or 20 miles N.W. of Susa, and to have sent a branch east of the Susa ruins, which absorbed the Shapur, a small tributary of the Dizful stream, and ran into the Kuran a little above Ahwaz. The remains of the old channel are still to be traced; and its existence explains the confusion, observable in ancient times, between the Kerkhah and the Kuran, to each of which streams, in certain parts of their course, we find the name Eulseus applied. The proper Eulseus was the eastern branch of the Kerkhah (Choaspes) from Pai Pul to Ahwaz; but the name was naturally extended both northwards to the Choaspes above Pai Pul and southwards to the Kuran below Ahwaz. The latter stream was, however, known also, both in its upper and its lower course, as the Pasitigris.

On the opposite side of the Empire the rivers were less considerable. Among the most important may be mentioned the Sajur, a tributary of the Euphrates, the Koweik, or river of Aleppo, the Orontes, or river of Antioch, the Litany, or river of Tyre, the Barada, or river of Damascus, and the Jordan, with its tributaries, the Jabbok and the Hieromax.

The Sajur rises from two principle sources on the southern flanks of Amanus, which, after running a short distance, unite a little to the east of Ain-Tab. The course of the stream from the point of junction is south-east. In this direction it flows in a somewhat tortuous channel between two ranges of hills for a distance of about 30 miles to Tel Khalid, a remarkable conical hill crowned by ruins. Here it receives an important affluent-the Keraskat-from the west, and becomes suitable for boat navigation. At the same time its course changes, and runs eastward for about 12 miles; after which the stream again inclines to the south, and keeping an E.S.E.

direction for 14 or 15 miles, enters the Euphrates by five mouths in about lat. 36° 37'. The course of the river measures probably about 65 miles.

The Koweik, or river of Aleppo (the Chalus of Xenophon), rises in the hills south of Ain-Tab. Springing from two sources, one of which is known as the Baloklu-Su, or "Fish River," it flows at first eastward, as if intending to join the Euphrates. On reaching the plain of Aleppo, however, near Sayyadok-Koi, it receives a tributary from the north, which gives its course a southern inclination; and from this point it proceeds in a south and south-westerly direction, winding along the shallow bed which it has scooped in the Aloppo plain, a distance of 60 miles, past Aleppo to Kinnisrin, near the foot of the Jebel-el-Sis. Here its further progress southward is barred, and it is forced to turn to the east along the foot of the mountain, which it skirts for eight or ten miles, finally entering the small lake or marsh of El Melak, in which it loses itself after a source of about 80 miles.

The Orontes, the great river of Assyria, rises in the Buka'a —the deep valley known to the ancients as Coele-Syria Proper-springing from a number of small brooks, which flow down from the Antilibanus range between lat. 34° 5' and lat. 34° 12'. Its most remote source is near Yunin, about seven mites N.N.E. of Baalbek. The stream flows at first N.W. by W. into the plain, on reaching which it turns at a right-angle to the northeast, and skirts the foot of the Antilibanus range as far as Lebweh, where, being joined by a larger stream from the southeast,130 it takes its direction and flows N.W. and then N. across the plain to the foot of Lebanon. Here it receives the waters of a much more abundant fountain, which wells out from the roots of that range, and is regarded by the Orientals as the true "head of the stream." Thus increased the river flows northwards for a short space, after which it turns to the northeast, and runs in a deep cleft along the base of Lebanon, pursuing this direction for 15 or 16 miles to a point beyond Ribleh, nearly in lat. 34° 30'. Here the course of the river again changes, becoming slightly west of north to the Lake of Hems (Buheiret-Hems), which is nine or ten miles below Ribleh. Issuing from the Lake of Hems about lat. 34° 43', the Orontes once more flows to the north east, and in five or six miles reaches Hems itself, which it leaves on its right bank. It then flows for twenty miles nearly due north, after which, on approaching Hama (Hamath), it makes a slight bend to the east round the foot of Jebel Erbayn, and then entering the rich pasture country of El-Ghab' runs north-west and north to the "Iron Bridge" (Jisr Hadid), in lat. 36° 11'. Its course thus far has been nearly parallel with the coast of the Mediterranean, and has lain between two ranges of mountains, the more western of which has shut it out from the sea. At Jisr Hadid the western mountains come to an end, and the Orontes, sweeping round their base, runs first west and then south-west down the broad valley of Antioch, in the midst of the most lovely scenery, to the coast, which it reaches a little above the 36th parallel, in long. 35° 55'. The course of the Orontes, exclusive of lesser windings, is about 200 miles. It is a considerable stream almost from its source. At Hamah, more than a hundred miles from its mouth, it is crossed by a bridge of thirteen arches. At Antioch it is fifty yards in width, and runs rapidly. The natives now call it the Nahr-el-Asy, or "Rebel River," either from its running in an opposite direction to all other streams of the country, or (more probably) from its violence and impetuosity.

There is one tributary of the Orontes which deserves a cursory mention. This is the Kara Su, or "Black River," which reaches it from the Aga Denghis, or Bahr-el-Abiyad, about five miles below Jisr Hadid and four or five above Antioch. This stream brings into the Orontes the greater part of the water that is drained from the southern side of Amanus. It is formed by a union of two rivers, the upper Kara Su and the Afrin, which flow into the Aga Denghis (White Sea), or Lake of Antioch, from the north-west, the one entering it at its northern, the other at its eastern extremity. Both are considerable streams; and the Kara Su on issuing from the lake carries a greater body of water than the Orontes itself, and thus adds largely to the volume of that stream in its lower course from the point of junction to the Mediterranean.

The Litany, or river of Tyre, rises from a source at no great distance from the head springs of the Orontes. The almost imperceptible watershed of the Buka'a runs between Yunin and Baalbek, a few miles north of the latter; and when it is once passed, the drainage of the water is southwards. The highest permanent fountain of the southern stream seems to be a small lake near Tel Hushben, which lies about six miles to the south-west of the Baalbek ruins. Springing from this source the Litany flows along the lower Buka'a in a direction which is generally a little west of south, receiving on either side a number of streamlets and rills from Libanus and Anti-libanus, and giving out in its turn numerous canals for irrigation, which fertilize the thirsty soil. As the stream descends with numerous windings, but still with the same general course, the valley of the Buka'a contracts more and more, till finally it terminates in a gorge, down which thunders the Litany—a gorge a thousand feet or more in depth, and so narrow that in one place it is actually bridged over by masses of rock which have fallen from the jagged sides. Narrower and deeper grows the gorge, and the river chafes and foams through it, gradually working itself round to the west, and so clearing a way through the very roots of Lebanon to the low coast tract, across which it meanders slowly, as if wearied with its long struggle, before finally emptying itself into the sea. The course of the Litany may be roughly estimated at from 70 to 75 miles.

The Barada, or river of Damascus, rises in the plain of Zebdany-the very centre of the Antilibanus. It has its real permanent source in a small nameless lake in the lower part of the plain, about lat. 33° 41'; but in winter it is fed by streams flowing from the valley above, especially by one which rises in lat. 33° 46', near the small hamlet of Ain Hawar. The course of the Barada from the small lake is at first towards the east; but it soon sweeps round and flows-southward for about four miles to the lower end of the plain, after which it again turns to the east and enters a romantic glen, running between high cliffs, and cutting through the main ridge of the Antilibanus between the Zebdany plain and Suk, the Abila of the ancients. From Suk the river flows through a narrow but lovely valley, in a course which has a general direction of south-east, past Ain Fijoh (where its waters are greatly increased), through a series of gorges and glens, to the point where the roots of the Antilibanus sink down upon the plain, when it bursts forth from the mountains and scatters. Channels are drawn from it on either side, and its waters are spread far and wide over the Merj, which it covers with fine trees and splendid herbage.

One branch passes right through the city, cutting it in half. Others irrigate the gardens and orchards both to the north and to the south. Beyond the town the tendency to division still continues. The river, weakened greatly through the irrigation, separates into three main channels, which flow with divergent courses towards the east, and terminate in two large swamps or lakes, the Bahret-esh-Shurkiyeh and the Bahret-el-Kibli-yeh, at a distance of sixteen or seventeen miles from the city. The Barada is a short stream, its entire course from the plain of Zebdany not much exceeding forty miles.

The Jordan is commonly regarded as flowing from two sources in the Huleh or plain immediately above Lake Merom, one at Banias (the ancient Paneas), the other at Tel-el-Kady, which marks the site of Laish or Dan. But the true highest present source of the river is the spring near Hasbeiya, called Nebaes-Hasbany, or Eas-en-Neba. This spring rises in the torrent-course known as the Wady-el-Teim, which descends from the north-western flank of Hermon, and runs nearly parallel with the great gorge of the Litany, having a direction from north-east to south-west. The water wells forth in abundance from the foot of a volcanic bluff, called Eas-el-Anjah, lying directly north of Hasbeiya, and is immediately used to turn a mill. The course of the streamlet is very slightly west of south down the Wady to the Huleh plain, where it is joined, and multiplied sevenfold, by the streams from Banais and Tel-el-Kady, becoming at once worthy of the name of river. Hence it runs almost due south to the Merom lake, which it enters in lat. 33° 7', through a reedy and marshy tract which it is difficult to penetrate. Issuing from Merom in lat. 33° 3', the Jordan flows at first sluggishly southward to "Jacob's Bridge," passing which, it proceeds in the same direction, with a much swifter current down the depressed and narrow cleft between Merom and Tiberias, descending at the rate of fifty feet in a mile, and becoming (as has been said) a sort of "continuous waterfall." Before reaching Tiberias its course bends slightly to the west of south for about two miles, and it pours itself into that "sea" in about lat. 32° 53'. Quitting the sea in lat. 32° 42', it finally enters the track called the Ghor, the still lower chasm or cleft which intervenes between Tiberias and the upper end of the Dead Sea. Here the descent of the stream becomes comparatively gentle, not much exceeding three feet per mile; for though the direct distance between the two lakes is less than seventy miles, and the entire fall above 600 feet, which would seem to give a descent of nine or ten feet a mile, yet, as the course of the river throughout this part of its career is tortuous in the extreme, the fall is really not greater than above indicated. Still it is sufficient to produce as many as twenty-seven rapids, or at the rate of one to every seven miles. In this part of its course the Jordan receives two important tributaries, each of which seems to deserve a few words.

The Jarmuk, or Sheriat-el-Mandhur, anciently the Hiero-max, drains the water, not only from Gaulonitis or Jaulan, the country immediately east and south-east of the sea of Tiberias, but also from almost the whole of the Hauran. At its mouth it is 130 feet wide, and in the winter it brings down a great body of water into the Jordan. In summer, however, it shrinks up into an inconsiderable brook, having no more remote sources than the perennial springs at Mazarib, Dilly, and one or two other places on the plateau of Jaulan. It runs through a fertile country, and has generally a deep course far below the surface of the plain; ere falling into the Jordan it makes its way through a wild ravine, between rugged cliffs of basalt, which are in places upwards of a hundred feet in height.

The Zurka, or Jabbok, is a stream of the same character with the Hieromax, but of inferior dimensions and importance. It drains a considerable portion of the land of Gilead, but has no very remote sources, and in summer only carries water through a few miles of its lower course. In winter, on the contrary, it is a roaring stream with a strong current, and sometimes cannot be forded. The ravine through which it flows is narrow, deep, and in some places wild. Throughout nearly its whole course it is fringed by thickets of cane and oleander, while above, its banks are clothed with forests of oak.

The Jordan receives the Hieromax about four or five miles below the point where it issues from the Sea of Tiberias, and the Jabbok about half-way between that lake and the Dead Sea. Augmented by these streams, and others of less importance from the mountains on either side, it becomes a river of considerable size, being opposite Beth-shan (Beisan) 140 feet wide, and three feet deep, and averaging, in its lower course, a width of ninety with a depth of eight or nine feet. Its entire course, from the fountain near Hasbeiya to the Dead Sea, including the passage of the two lakes through which it flows, is, if we exclude meanders, about 130, if we include them, 360 miles. It is calculated to pour into the Dead Sea 6,090,000 tons of water daily.

Besides these rivers the Babylonian territory comprised a number of important lakes. Of these some of the more eastern have been described in a former volume: as the Bahr-i-Nedjif in Lower Chaldæa, and the Lake of Khatouniyeh in the tract between the Sinjar and the Khabour. It was chiefly, however, towards the west that sheets of water abounded: the principal of these were the Sabakhah, the Bahr-el-Melak, and the Lake of Antioch in Upper Syria; the Bahr-el-Kades, or Lake of Hems, in the central region; and the Damascus lakes, the Lake of Merom, the Sea of Galilee or Tiberias, and the Dead Sea, in the regions lying furthest to the south. Of these the greater number were salt, and of little value, except as furnishing the salt of commerce; but four-the Lake of Antioch, the Bahr-el-Kades, the Lake Merom, and the Sea of Galilee-were fresh-water basins lying upon the courses of streams which ran through them; and these not only diversified the scenery by their clear bright aspect, but were of considerable value to the inhabitants, as furnishing them with many excellent sorts of fish.

Of the salt lakes the most eastern was the Sabakhah. This is a basin of long and narrow form, lying on and just below the 36th parallel. It is situated on the southern route from Balis to Aleppo, and is nearly equally distant between the two places. Its length is from twelve to thirteen miles; and its width, where it is broadest, is about five miles. It receives from the north the waters of the Nahr-el-Dhahab, or "Golden River" (which has by some been identified with the Daradax of Xenophon), and from the west two or three insignificant streams, which empty themselves into its western extremity. The lake produces a large quantity of salt, especially after wet seasons, which is collected and sold by the inhabitants of the surrounding country.

The Bahr-el-Molak, the lake which absorbs the Koweik, or river of Aleppo, is less than twenty miles distant from Lake Sabakhah, which it very much resembles in its general character. Its ordinary length is about nine miles, and its width three or four; but in winter it is greatly swollen by the rains, and at that time it spreads out so widely that its circumference sometimes exceeds fifty miles. Much salt is drawn from its bed in the dry season, and a large part of Syria is hence supplied with the commodity. The lake is covered with small islands, and greatly frequented by aquatic birds-geese, ducks, flamingoes, and the like.

The lakes in the neighborhood of Damascus are three in number, and are all of a very similar type. They are indeterminate in size and shape, changing with the wetness or dryness of the season; and it is possible that sometimes they may be all united in one. The most northern, which is called the Bahret-esh-Shurkiyeh, receives about half the surplus water of the Barada, together with some streamlets from the outlying ranges of Antilibanus towards the north. The central one, called the Bahret-el-Kibliyeh, receives the rest of the Barada water, which enters it by three or four branches on its northern and western sides. The most southern, known as Bahret-Hijaneh, is the receptacle for the stream of the Awaaj, and takes also the water from the northern parts of the Ledjah, or region of Argob. The three lakes are in the same line —a line which runs from N.N.E. to S.S.W. They are, or at least were recently, separated by tracts of dry land from two to four miles broad. Dense thickets of tall reeds surround them, and in summer almost cover their surface. Like the Bahr-el-Melak, they are a home for water-fowl, which flock to them in enormous numbers.

By far the largest and most important of the salt lakes is the Great Lake of the South-the Bahr Lut ("Sea of Lot"), or Dead Sea. This sheet of water, which has always attracted the special notice and observation of travellers, has of late years been scientifically surveyed by officers of the American navy; and its shape, its size, and even its depth, are thus known with accuracy. The Dead Sea is of an oblong form, and would be of a very regular contour, were it not for a remarkable projection from its eastern shore near its southern extremity. In this place, a long and low peninsula, shaped like a human foot, projects into the lake, filling up two thirds of its width, and thus dividing the expanse of water into two portions, which are connected by a long and somewhat narrow passage. The entire length of the sea, from north to south, is 46 miles: its greatest width, between its eastern and its western shores, is 101 miles. The whole area is estimated at 250 geographical square miles. Of this space 174 square miles belong to the northern portion of the lake (the true "Sea"), 29 to the narrow channel, and 46 to the southern portion, which has been called "the back-water," or "the lagoon."

The most remarkable difference between the two portions of the lake is the contrast they present as to depth. While the depth of the northern portion is from 600 feet, at a short distance from the mouth of the Jordan, to 800, 1000, 1200, and even 1300 feet, further down, the depth of the lagoon is nowhere more than 12 or 13 feet; and in places it is so shallow that it has been found possible, in some seasons, to ford the whole way across from one side to the other. The peculiarities of the Dead Sea, as compared with other lakes, are its depression below the sea-level, its buoyancy, and its extreme saltness. The degree of the depression is not yet certainly known; but there is reason to believe that it is at least as much at 1300 feet, whereas no other lake is known to be depressed more than 570 feet. The buoyancy and the saltness are not so wholly unparalleled. The waters of Lake Urumiyeh are probably as salt and as buoyant; those of Lake Elton in the steppe east of the Wolga, and of certain other Russian lakes, appear to be even salter. But with these few exceptions (if they are exceptions), the Dead Sea water must be pronounced to be the heaviest and saltest water known to us. More than one fourth of its weight is solid matter held in solution. Of this solid matter nearly one third is common salt, which is more than twice as much as is contained in the waters of the ocean.

Of the fresh-water lakes the largest and most important is the Sea of Tiberias. This sheet of water is of an oval shape, with an axis, like that of the Dead Sea, very nearly due north and south. Its greatest length is about thirteen and its greatest width about six miles. Its extreme depth, so far as has been ascertained, is 27 fathoms, or 165 feet. The Jordan flows into its upper end turbid and muddy, and issues forth at its southern extremity clear and pellucid. It receives also the waters of a considerable number of small streams and springs, some of which are warm and brackish; yet its own water is always sweet, cool, and transparent, and, having everywhere a shelving pebbly beach, has a bright sparkling appearance. The banks are lofty, and in general destitute of verdure. What exactly is the amount of depression below the level of the Mediterranean remains still, to some extent, uncertain; but it is probably not much less than 700 feet. Now, as formerly, the lake produces an abundance of fish, which are pronounced, by those who have partaken of them, to be "delicious."

Nine miles above the Sea of Tiberias, on the course of the same stream, is the far smaller basin known now as the Bahr-el Huleh, and anciently (perhaps) as Merom. This is a mountain tarn, varying in size as the season is wet or dry, but never apparently more than about seven miles long, by five or six broad. It is situated at the lower extremity of the plain called Huleh, and is almost entirely surrounded by flat marshy ground, thickly set with reeds and canes, which make the lake itself almost unapproachable. The depth of the Huleh is not known. It is a favorite resort of aquatic birds, and is said to contain an abundant supply of fish.

The Bahr-el-Kades, or Lake of Hems, lies on the course of the Orontes, about 139 miles N.N.E. of Merom, and nearly the same distance south of the Lake of Antioch. It is a small sheet of water, not more than six or eight miles long, and only two or three wide, running in the same direction with the course of the river, which here turns from north to north-east. According to Abulfeda and some other writers, it is mainly, if not wholly, artificial, owing its origin to a dam or embankment across the stream, which is from four to five hundred yards in length, and about twelve or fourteen feet high. In Abulfeda's time the construction of the embankment was ascribed to Alexander the Great, and the lake consequently was not regarded as having had any existence in Babylonian times; but traditions of this kind are little to be trusted, and it is quite possible that the work above mentioned, constructed apparently with a view to irrigation, may really belong to a very much earlier age.

Finally, in Northern Syria, 115 miles north of the Bahr-el-Kades, and about 60 miles N.W.W. of the Bahr-el-Melak, is the Bahr-el-Abyad (White Lake), or Sea of Antioch. This sheet of water is a parallelogram, the angles of which face the cardinal points: in its greater diameter it extends somewhat more than ten miles, while it is about seven miles across. Its depth on the western side, where it approaches the mountains, is six or eight feet; but elsewhere it is generally more shallow, not exceeding three or four feet. It lies in a marshy plain called El-Umk, and is thickly fringed with reeds round the whole of its circumference. From the silence of antiquity, some writers have imagined that it did not exist in ancient times; but the observations of scientific travellers are opposed to this theory. The lake abounds with fish of several kinds, and the fishery attracts and employs a considerable number of the natives who dwell near it.

The Sea of Antioch, from the East.

Besides these lakes, there were contained within the limits of the Empire a number of petty tarns, which do not merit particular description. Such were the Bahr-el-Taka, and other small lakes on the right bank of the middle Orontes, the Birket-el-Limum in the Lebanon, and the Birket-er-Eam on the southern flank of Hermon. It is unnecessary, however, to pursue this subject any further. But a few words must be added on the chief cities of the Empire, before this chapter is brought to a conclusion.

The cities of the Empire may be divided into those of the dominant country and those of the provinces. Those of the dominant country were, for the most part, identical with the towns already described as belonging to the ancient Chaldaea, Besides Babylon itself, there flourished in the Babylonian period the cities of Borsippa, Duraba, Sippara or Sepharvaim, Opis, Psittace, Cutha, Orchoe or Erech, and Diridotis or Teredon. The sites of most of those have been described in the first volume; but it remains to state briefly the positions of some few which were either new creations or comparatively undistinguished in the earlier times.

Opis, a town of sufficient magnitude to attract the attention of Herodotus, was situated on the left or east bank of the Tigris, near the point where the Diyaleh or Gyndes joined the main river. Its position was south of the Gyndes embouchure, and it might be reckoned as lying upon either river. The true name of the place-that which it bears in the cuneiform inscriptions-was Hupiya; and its site is probably marked by the ruins at Khafaji, near Baghdad, which place is thought to retain, in a corrupted form, the original appellation. Psittace or Sitace, the town which gave name to the province of Sittacene, was in the near neighborhood of Opis, lying on the same side of the Tigris, but lower down, at least as low as the modern fort of the Zobeid chief. Its exact site has not been as yet discovered. Teredon, or Diriaotis, appears to have been first founded by Nebuchadnezzar. It lay on the coast of the Persian Gulf, a little west of the mouth of the Euphrates, and protected by a quay, or a breakwater, from the high tides that rolled in from the Indian Ocean. There is great difficulty in identifying its site, owing to the extreme uncertainty as to the exact position of the coast-line, and the course of the river, in the time of Nebuchadnezzar. Probably it should be sought about Zobair, or a little further inland..

The chief provincial cities were Susa and Badaca in Susiana; Anat, Sirki, and Carchemish, on the Middle Euphrates; Sidikan on the Khabour; Harran on the Bilik; Hamath, Damascus, and Jerusalem, in Inner Syria; Tyre, Sidon, Ashdod, Ascalon, and Gaza, upon the coast. Of these, Susa was undoubtedly the most important; indeed, it deserves to be regarded as the second city of the Empire. Here, between the two arms of the Choaspes, on a noble and well-watered plain, backed at the distance of twenty-five miles by a lofty mountain range, the fresh breezes from which tempered the summer heats, was the ancient palace of the Kissian kings, proudly placed upon a lofty platform or mound, and commanding a wide prospect of the rich pastures at its base, which extended northwards to the roots of the hills, and in every other direction as far as the eye could reach. Clustered at the foot of the palace mound, more especially on its eastern side, lay the ancient town, the foundation of the traditional Memnon who led an army to the defence of Troy. The pure and sparkling water of the Choaspes —a drink fit for kings-flowed near, while around grew palms, konars, and lemon-trees, the plain beyond waving with green grass and golden corn. It may be suspected that the Babylonian kings, who certainly maintained a palace at this place, and sent high officers of their court to "do their business" there, made it their occasional residence, exchanging, in summer and early autumn, the heats and swamps of Babylon for the comparatively dry and cool region at the base of the Lurish hills. But, however, this may have been, at any rate Susa, long the capital of a kingdom little inferior to Babylon itself, must have been the first of the provincial cities, surpassing all the rest at once in size and in magnificence. Among the other cities, Carchemish on the Upper Euphrates, Tyre upon the Syrian coast, and Ashdod on the borders of Egypt, held the highest place. Carchemish, which has been wrongly identified with Circesium, lay certainly high up the river, and most likely occupied a site some distance to the north of Balis, which is in lat. 36° nearly. It was the key of Syria on the east, commanding the ordinary passage of the Euphrates, and being the only great city in this quarter. Tyre, which had by this time surpassed its rival, Sidon, was the chief of all the maritime towns; and its possession gave the mastery of the Eastern Mediterranean to the power which could acquire and maintain it. Ashdod was the key of Syria upon the south, being a place of great strength, and commanding the coast route between Palestine and Egypt, which was usually pursued by armies. It is scarcely too much to say that the possession of Ashdod, Tyre, and Carchemish, involved the lordship of Syria, which could not be permanently retained except by the occupation of those cities.

The countries by which the Babylonian Empire was bounded were Persia on the east, Media and her dependencies on the north, Arabia on the south, and Egypt at the extreme south-west. Directly to the west she had no neighbor, her territory being on that side washed by the Mediterranean.

Of Persia, which must be described at length in the next volume, since it was the seat of Empire during the Fifth Monarchy, no more need be said here than that it was for the most part a rugged and sterile country, apt to produce a brave and hardy race, but incapable of sustaining a large population. A strong barrier separated it from the great Mesopotamian lowland; and the Babylonians, by occupying a few easily defensible passes, could readily prevent a Persian army from debouching on their fertile plains. On the other hand, the natural strength of the region is so great that in the hands of brave and active men its defence is easy; and the Babylonians were not likely, if an aggressive spirit led to their pressing eastward, to make any serious impression in this quarter, or ever greatly to advance their frontier.

To Media, the power which bordered her upon the north, Babylonia, on the contrary, lay wholly open. The Medes, possessing Assyria and Armenia, with the Upper Tigris valley, and probably the Mons Masius, could at any time, with the greatest ease, have marched armies into the low country, and resumed the contest in which Assyria was engaged for so many hundred years with the great people of the south. On this side nature had set no obstacles; and, if danger threatened, resistance had to be made by means of those artificial works which are specially suited for flat countries. Long lines of wall, broad dykes, huge reservoirs, by means of which large tracts may be laid under water, form the natural resort in such a case; and to such defences as these alone, in addition to her armies, could Babylonia look in case of a quarrel with the Medes. On this side, however, she for many years felt no fear. Political arrangements and family ties connected her with the Median reigning house, and she looked to her northern neighbor as an ally upon whom she might depend for aid, rather than as a rival whose ambitious designs were to be watched and baffled.

Babylonia lay open also on the side of Arabia. Here, however, the nature of the country is such that population must be always sparse; and the habits of the people are opposed to that political union which can alone make a race really formidable to others. Once only in their history, under the excitement of a religious frenzy, have the Arabs issued forth from the great peninsula on an errand of conquest. In general they are content to vex and harass without seriously alarming their neighbors. The vast space and arid character of the peninsula are adverse to the collection and the movement of armies; the love of independence cherished by the several tribes indisposes them to union; the affection for the nomadic life, which is strongly felt, disinclines them to the occupation of conquests. Arabia, as a a conterminous power, is troublesome, but rarely dangerous: one section of the nation may almost always be played off against another: if "their hand is against every man," "every man's hand" is also "against them;" blood-feuds divide and decimate their tribes, which are ever turning their swords against each other; their neighbors generally wish them ill, and will fall upon them, if they can take them at a disadvantage; it is only under very peculiar circumstances, such as can very rarely exist, that they are likely even to attempt anything more serious than a plundering inroad. Babylonia consequently, though open to attack on the side of the south as well as on that of the north, had little to fear from either quarter. The friendliness of her northern neighbor, and the practical weakness of her southern one, were equal securities against aggression; and thus on her two largest and most exposed frontiers the Empire dreaded no attack.

But it was otherwise in the far south-west. Here the Empire bordered upon Egypt, a rich and populous country, which at all times covets Syria, and is often strong enough to seize and hold it in possession. The natural frontier is moreover weak, no other barrier separating between Africa and Asia than a narrow desert, which has never yet proved a serious obstacle to an army. From the side of Egypt, if from no other quarter, Babylonia might expect to have trouble. Here she inherited from her predecessor, Assyria, an old hereditary feud, which might at any time break out into active hostility. Here was an ancient, powerful, and well-organized kingdom upon her borders, with claims upon that portion of her territory which it was most difficult for her to defend effectively. By seas and by land equally the strip of Syrian coast lay open to the arms of Egypt, who was free to choose her time, and pour her hosts into the country when the attention of Babylon was directed to some other quarter. The physical and political circumstances alike pointed to hostile transactions between Babylon and her south-western neighbor. Whether destruction would come from this quarter, or from some other, it would have been impossible to predict. Perhaps, on the whole, it may be said that Babylon might have been expected to contend successfully with Egypt-that she had little to fear from Arabia-that against Persia Proper it might have been anticipated that she would be able to defend herself-but that she lay at the mercy of Media. The Babylonian Empire was in truth an empire upon sufferance. From the time of its establishment with the consent of the Medes, the Modes might at any time have destroyed it. The dynastic tie alone prevented this result. When that tie was snapped, and when moreover, by the victories of Cyrus, Persian enterprise succeeded to the direction of Median power, the fate of Babylon was sealed. It was impossible for the long straggling Empire of the south, lying chiefly in low, flat, open regions, to resist for any considerable time the great kingdom of the north, of the high plateau, and of the mountain-chains.

Chapter II. Climate and Productions

....Πεδίον περιωσιον ένθα τε πολλοι
Ακροκομοι φοίνικες επηρεφεες πεφυασι
Και μην και χρυσοιο φέρει χαριεστερον άλλο,
Υγρής βηρύλλου γλαυκήν λίθον, η περί χωρών
Φύεται, εν προβολής, οφιητίδος ενδοθι πετρης.

Dionys. Perieg. 11. 1009-1013.

Εστί δε χωρεών αυτή απασών μακρό αρίστη τον ημείς ιδμεν Δημητρος καρπών εκφέρειν. —Herod, i. 193.

The Babylonian Empire, lying as it did between the thirtieth and thirty-seventh parallels of north latitude, and consisting mostly of comparatively low countries, enjoyed a climate which was, upon the whole, considerably warmer than that of Media, and less subject to extreme variations. In its more southern parts-Susiana, Chaldaea (or Babylonia Proper), Philistia, and Edom —-the intensity of the summer heat must have been great; but the winters were mild and of short duration. In the middle regions of Central Mesopotamia, the Euphrates valley, the Palmyrene, Coele-Syria, Judaea, and Phoenicia, while the winters were somewhat colder and longer, the summer warmth was more tolerable. Towards the north, along the flanks of Masius, Taurus, and Amanus, a climate more like that of eastern Media prevailed, the summers being little less hot than those of the middle region, while the winters were of considerable severity. A variety of climate thus existed, but a variety within somewhat narrow limits. The region was altogether hotter and drier than is usual in the same latitude. The close proximity of the great Arabian desert, the small size of the adjoining seas, the want of mountains within the region having any great elevation, and the general absence of timber, combined to produce an amount of heat and dryness scarcely known elsewhere outside the tropics.

Detailed accounts of the temperature, and of the climate generally, in the most important provinces of the Empire, Babylonia and Mesopotamia Proper, have been already given, and on these points the reader is referred to the first volume. With regard to the remaining provinces, it may be noticed, in the first place, that the climate of Susiana differs but very slightly from that of Babylonia, the region to which it is adjacent. The heat in summer is excessive, the thermometer, even in the hill country, at an elevation of 5000 feet, standing often at 107° Fahr. in the shade. The natives construct for themselves serdaubs, or subterranean apartments, in which they live during the day, thus somewhat reducing the temperature, but probably never bringing it much below 100 degrees. They sleep at night in the open air on the flat roofs of their houses. So far as there is any difference of climate at this season between Susiana and Babylonia, it is in favor of the former. The heat, though scorching, is rarely oppressive; and not unfrequently a cool, invigorating breeze sets in from the mountains, which refreshes both mind and body. The winters are exceedingly mild, snow being unknown on the plains, and rare on the mountains, except at a considerable elevation. At this time, however-from December to the end of March-rain falls in tropical abundance; and occasionally there are violent hail-storms, which inflict serious injury on the crops. The spring-time in Susiana is delightful. Soft airs fan the cheek, laden with the scent of flowers; a carpet of verdure is spread over the plains; the sky is cloudless, or overspread with a thin gauzy veil; the heat of the sun is not too great; the rivers run with full banks and fill the numerous canals; the crops advance rapidly towards perfection; and on every side a rich luxuriant growth cheers the eye of the traveller.

On the opposite side of the Empire, in Syria and Palestine, a moister, and on the whole a cooler climate prevails. In Lebanon and Anti-Lebanon there is a severe winter, which lasts from October to April; much snow falls, and the thermometer often marks twenty or thirty degrees of frost. On the flanks of the mountain ranges, and in the highlands of Upper and Coele-Syria, of Damascus, Samaria, and Judæa, the cold is considerably less; but there are intervals of frost; snow falls, though it does not often remain long upon the ground; and prolonged chilling rains make the winter and early spring unpleasant. In the low regions, on the other hand, in the *Shephelah*, the plain of Sharon, the Phoenician coast tract, the lower valley of the Orontes, and again in the plain of Esdraelon and the remarkable depression from the Merom lake to the Dead Sea, the winters are exceedingly mild; frost and snow are unknown; the lowest temperature is produced by cold rains and fogs, which do not bring the thermometer much below 40°. During the summer these low regions, especially the Jordan valley or Ghor, are excessively hot, the heat being ordinarily of that moist kind which is intolerably oppressive. The upland plains and mountain flanks experience also a high temperature, but there the heat is of a drier character, and is not greatly complained of; the nights even in summer are cold, the dews being often heavy; cool winds blow occasionally, and though the sky is for months without a cloud, the prevailing heat produces no injurious effects on those who are exposed to it. In Lebanon and Anti-Lebanon the heat is of course still less; refreshing breezes blow almost constantly; and the numerous streams and woods give a sense of coolness beyond the markings of the thermometer.

There is one evil, however, to which almost the whole Empire must have been subject. Alike in the east and in the west, in Syria and Palestine, no less than in Babylonia Proper and Susiana, there are times when a fierce and scorching wind prevails for days together—a wind whose breath withers the herbage and is unspeakably depressing to man. Called in the east the Sherghis, and in the west the Khamsin, this fiery sirocco comes laden with fine particles of heated sand, which at once raise the temperature and render the air unwholesome to breathe. In Syria these winds occur commonly in the spring, from February to April; but in Susiana and Babylonia the time for them is the height of summer. They blow from various quarters, according to the position, with respect to Arabia, occupied by the different provinces. In Palestine the worst are from the east, the direction in which the desert is nearest; in Lower Babylonia they are from the south; in Susiana from the west or the north-west. During their continuance the air is darkened, a lurid glow is cast over the earth, the animal world pines and droops, vegetation languishes, and, if the traveller cannot obtain shelter, and the wind continues, he may sink and die under its deleterious influence.

The climate of the entire tract included within the limits of the Empire was probably much the same in ancient times as in our own days. In the low alluvial plains indeed near the Persian Gulf it is probable that vegetation was anciently more abundant, the date-palm being cultivated much more extensively then than at present; and so far it might appear reasonable to conclude that the climate of that region must have been moister and cooler than it now is. But if we may judge by Strabo's account of Susiana, where the climatic conditions were nearly the same as in Babylonia, no important change can have taken place, for Strabo not only calls the climate of Susiana "fiery and scorching," but says that in Susa, during the height of summer, if a lizard or a snake tried to cross the street about noon-day, he was baked to death before accomplishing half the distance. Similarly on the west, though there is reason to believe that Palestine is now much more denuded of timber than it was formerly, and its climate should therefore be both warmer and drier, yet it has been argued with great force from the identity of the modern with the ancient vegetation, that in reality there can have been no considerable change. If then there has been such permanency of climate in the two regions where the greatest alteration seems to have taken place in the circumstances whereby climate is usually affected, it can scarcely be thought that elsewhere any serious change has been brought about.

The chief vegetable productions of Babylonia Proper in ancient times are thus enumerated by Berosus. "The land of the Babylonians," he says, "produces wheat as an indigenous plant," and has also barley, and lentils, and vetches, and sesame; the banks of the streams and the marshes supply edible roots, called gongoe, which have the taste of barley-cakes. Palms, too, grow in the country, and apples, and fruit-trees of various kinds. Wheat, it will be observed, and barley are placed first, since it was especially as a grain country that Babylonia was celebrated. The testimonies of Herodotus, Theophrastus, Strabo, and Pliny as to the enormous returns which the Babylonian farmers obtained from their corn lands have been already cited. No such fertility is known anywhere in modern times; and, unless the accounts are grossly exaggerated, we must ascribe it, in part, to the extraordinary vigor of a virgin soil, a deep and rich alluvium; in part, perhaps, to a peculiar adaptation of the soil to the wheat plant, which the providence of God made to grow spontaneously in this region, and nowhere else, so far as we know, on the whole face of the earth.

Besides wheat, it appears that barley, millet, and lentils were cultivated for food, while vetches were grown for beasts, and sesame for the sake of the oil which can be expressed from its seed. All grew luxuriantly, and the returns of the barley in particular are stated at a fabulous amount. But the production of first necessity in Babylonia was the date-palm, which flourished in great abundance throughout the region, and probably furnished the chief food of the greater portion of the inhabitants. The various uses to which it was applied have been stated in the first volume, where a representation of its mode of growth has been also given.

In the adjoining country of Susiana, or at any rate in the alluvial portion of it, the principal products of the earth seem to have been nearly the same as in Babylonia, while the fecundity of the soil was but little less. Wheat and barley returned to the sower a hundred or even two hundred fold. The date-palm grew plentifully, more especially in the vicinity of the towns. Other trees also were common, as probably konars, acacias, and poplars, which are still found scattered in tolerable abundance over the plain country. The neighboring mountains could furnish good timber of various kinds; but it appears that the palm was the tree chiefly used for building. If we may judge the past by the present, we may further suppose that Susiana produced fruits in abundance; for modern travellers tell us that there is not a fruit known in Persia which does not thrive in the province of Khuzistan.

Along the Euphrates valley to a considerable distance-at least as far as Anah (or Hena) —the character of the country resembles that of Babylonia and Susiana, and the products cannot have been very different. About Anah the date-palm begins to fail, and the olive first makes its appearance. Further up a chief fruit is the mulberry. Still higher, in northern Mesopotamia, the mulberry is comparatively rare, but its place is supplied by the walnut, the vine, and the pistachio-nut. This district produces also good crops of grain, and grows oranges, pomegranates, and the commoner kinds of fruit abundantly.

Across the Euphrates, in Northern Syria, the country is less suited for grain crops; but trees and shrubs of all kinds grow luxuriantly, the pasture is excellent, and much of the land is well adapted for the growth of cotton. The Assyrian kings cut timber frequently in this tract; and here are found at the present day enormous planes, thick forests of oak, pine, and ilex, walnuts, willows, poplars, ash-trees, birches, larches, and the carob or locust tree. Among wild shrubs are the oleander with its ruddy blossoms, the myrtle, the bay, the arbutus, the clematis, the juniper, and the honeysuckle; among cultivated fruit-trees, the orange, the pomegranate, the pistachio-nut, the vine, the mulberry, and the olive. The adis, an excellent pea, and the Lycoperdon, or wild potato, grow in the neighborhood of Aleppo. The castor-oil plant is cultivated in the plain of Edlib. Melons, cucumbers, and most of the ordinary vegetables are produced in abundance and of good quality everywhere.

In Southern Syria and Palestine most of the same forms of vegetation occur, with several others of quite a new character. These are due either to the change of latitude, or to the tropical heat of the Jordan and Dead Sea valley, or finally to the high elevation of Hermon, Lebanon, and Anti-Lebanon. The date-palm fringes the Syrian shore as high as Beyrut, and formerly flourished in the Jordan valley, where, however, it is not now seen, except in a few dwarfed specimens near the Tiberias lake. The banana accompanies the date along the coast, and even grows as far north as Tripoli. The prickly pear, introduced from America, has completely neutralized itself, and is in general request for hedging. The fig mulberry (or true sycamore), another southern form, is also common, and grows to a considerable size. Other denizens of warm climes, unknown in Northern Syria, are the jujube, the tamarisk, the elasagnus or wild olive, the gum-styrax plant (*Styrax officinalis*), the egg-plant, the Egyptian papyrus, the sugar-cane, the scarlet misletoe, the solanum that produces the "Dead Sea apple" (*Solanum Sodomceum*), the yellow-flowered acacia, and the liquorice plant. Among the forms due to high elevation are the famous Lebanon cedar, several oaks and juniper, the maple, berberry, jessamine, ivy, butcher's broom, a rhododendron, and the gum-tragacanth plant. The fruits additional to those of the north are dates, lemons, almonds, shaddocks, and limes.

The chief mineral products of the Empire seem to have been bitumen, with its concomitants, naphtha and petroleum, salt, sulphur, nitre, copper, iron, perhaps silver, and several sorts of precious stones. Bitumen was furnished in great abundance by the springs at Hit or Is, which were celebrated in the days of Herodotus; it was also procured from Ardericca (Kir-Ab), and probably from Earn Ormuz, in Susiana, and likewise from the Dead Sea. Salt was obtainable from the various lakes which had no outlet, as especially from the Sabakhab, the Bahr-el-Melak, the Dead Sea, and a small lake near Tadmor or Palmyra. The Dead Sea gave also most probably both sulphur and nitre, but the latter only in small quantities. Copper and iron seem to have been yielded by the hills of Palestine. Silver was perhaps a product of the Anti-Lebanon.

It may be doubted whether any gems were really found in Babylonia itself, which, being purely alluvial, possesses no stone of any kind. Most likely the sorts known as Babylonian came from the neighboring Susiana, whose unexplored mountains may possess many rich treasures. According to Dionysius, the bed of the Choaspes produced numerous agates, and it may well be that from the same quarter came that "beryl more precious than gold," and those "highly reputed sard," which Babylon seems to have exported to other countries. The western provinces may, however, very probably have furnished the gems which are ascribed to them, as amethysts, which are said to have been found in the neighborhood of Petra, alabaster, which came from near Damascus, and the cyanus, a kind of lapis-lazuli, which was a production of Phoenicia. No doubt the Babylonian love of gems caused the provinces to be carefully searched for stones; and it is not improbable that they yielded besides the varieties already named, and the other unknown kinds mentioned by Pliny, many, if not most, of the materials which we find to have been used for seals by the ancient people. These are, cornelian, rock-crystal, chalcedony, onyx, jasper, quartz, serpentine, sienite, haematite, green felspar, pyrites, loadstone, and amazon-stone.

Stone for building was absent from Babylonia Proper and the alluvial tracts of Susiana, but in the other provinces it abounded. The Euphrates valley could furnish stone at almost any point above Hit; the mountain regions of Susiana could supply it in whatever quantity might be required; and in the western provinces it was only too plentiful. Near to Babylonia the most common kind was limestone; but about Had-disah on the Euphrates there was also a gritty, silicious rock alternating with iron-stone, and in the Arabian Desert were sandstone and granite. Such stone as was used in Babylon itself, and in the other cities of the low country, probably either came down the Euphrates, or was brought by canals from the adjacent part of Arabia. The quantity, however, thus consumed was small, the Babylonians being content for most uses with the brick, of which their own territory gave them a supply practically inexhaustible.

The principal wild animals known to have inhabited the Empire in ancient times are the following: the lion, the panther or large leopard, the hunting leopard, the bear, the hyena, the wild ox, the buffalo (?), the wild ass, the stag, the antelope, the ibex or wild goat, the wild sheep, the wild boar, the wolf, the jackal, the fox, the hare, and the rabbit. Of these, the lion, leopard, bear, stag, wolf, jackal, and fox seem to have been very widely diffused, while the remainder were rarer, and, generally speaking, confined to certain localities. The wild ass was met with only in the dry parts of Mesopotamia, and perhaps of Syria, the buffalo and wild boar only in moist regions, along the banks of rivers or among marshes. The wild ox was altogether scarce; the wild sheep, the rabbit, and the hare, were probably not common.

To this list may be added as present denizens of the region, and therefore probably belonging to it in ancient times, the lynx, the wildcat, the ratel, the sable, the genet, the badger, the otter, the beaver, the polecat, the jerboa, the rat, the mouse, the marmot, the porcupine, the squirrel, and perhaps the alligator. Of these the commonest at the present day are porcupines, badgers, otters, rats, mice, and jerboas. The ratel, sable, and genet belong only to the north; the beaver is found nowhere but in the Khabour and middle Euphrates; the alligator, if a denizen of the region at all exists only in the Euphrates.

The chief birds of the region are eagles, vultures, falcons, owls, hawks, many kinds of crows, magpies, jackdaws, thrushes, blackbirds, nightingales, larks, sparrows, goldfinches, swallows, doves of fourteen kinds, francolins, rock partridges, gray partridges, black partridges, quails, pheasants, capercailzies, bustards, flamingoes, pelicans, cormorants, storks, herons, cranes, wild-geese, ducks, teal, kingfishers, snipes, woodcocks, the sand-grouse, the hoopoe, the green parrot, the becafico, the locust-bird, the humming-bird (?), and the bee-eater. The eagle, pheasant, capercailzie, quail, parrot, locust-bird, becafico, and humming-bird are rare; the remainder are all tolerably common. Besides these, we know that in ancient times ostriches were found within the limits of the Empire, though now they have retreated further south into the Great Desert of Arabia. Perhaps bitterns may also formerly have frequented some of the countries belonging to it, though they are not mentioned among the birds of the region by modern writers.

There is a bird of the heron species, or rather of a species between the heron and the stork, which seems to deserve a few words of special description. It is found chiefly in Northern Syria, in the plain of Aleppo and the districts watered by the Koweik and Sajur rivers. The Arabs call it Tair-el-Raouf, or "the magnificent." This bird is of a grayish-white, the breast white, the joints of the wings tipped with scarlet, and the under part of the beak scarlet, the upper part being of a blackish-gray. The beak is nearly five inches long, and two thirds of an inch thick. The circumference of the eye is red; the feet are of a deep yellow; and the bird in its general form strongly resembles the stork; but its color is darker. It is four feet high, and covers a breadth of nine feet when the wings are spread. The birds of this species are wont to collect in large flocks on the North Syrian rivers, and to arrange themselves in several rows across the streams where they are shallowest. Here they squat side by side, as close to one another as possible, and spread out their tails against the current, thus forming a temporary dam. The water drains off below them, and when it has reached its lowest point, at a signal from one of their number who from the bank watches the proceedings, they rise and swoop upon the fish, frogs, etc., which the lowering of the water has exposed to view.

Fish are abundant in the Chaldaean marshes, and in almost all the fresh-water lakes and rivers. The Tigris and Euphrates yield chiefly barbel and carp; but the former stream has also eels, trout, chub, shad-fish, siluruses, and many kinds which have no English names. The Koweik contains the Aleppo eel (*Ophidium masbacambahis*), a very rare variety; and in other streams of Northern Syria are found lampreys, bream, dace, and the black-fish (*Macropteronotus niger*), besides carp, trout, chub, and barbel. Chub, bream, and the silurus are taken in the Sea of Galilee. The black-fish is extremely abundant in the Bahr-el-Taka and the Lake of Antioch.

Among reptiles may be noticed, besides snakes, lizards, and frogs, which are numerous, the following less common species-iguanoes, tortoises of two kinds, chameleons, and monitors. Bats also were common in Babylonia Proper, where they grew to a great size. Of insects the most remarkable are scorpions, tarantulas, and locusts.

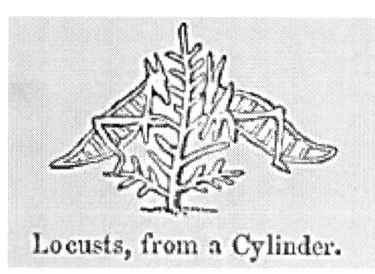

Locusts, from a Cylinder.

These last come suddenly in countless myriads with the wind, and, settling on the crops, rapidly destroy all the hopes of the husbandman, after which they strip the shrubs and trees of their leaves, reducing rich districts in an incredibly short space of time to the condition of howling wildernesses. If it were not for the locust-bird, which is constantly keeping down their numbers, these destructive insects would probably increase so as to ruin utterly the various regions exposed to their ravages.

The domestic animals employed in the countries which composed the Empire were, camels, horses, mules, asses, buffaloes, cows and oxen, goats, sheep, and dogs. Mules as well as horses seem to have been anciently used in war by the people of the more southern regions-by the Susianians at any rate, if not also by the Babylonians. Sometimes they were ridden; sometimes they were employed to draw carts or chariots.

Susianian mule (Koyunjik).

They were spirited and active animals, evidently of a fine breed, such as that for which Khuzistan is famous at the present day. The asses from which these mules were produced must also have been of superior quality, like the breed for which Baghdad is even now famous, The Babylonian horses are not likely to have been nearly so good; for this animal does not flourish in a climate which is at once moist and hot. Still, at any rate under the Persians, Babylonia seems to have been a great breeding-place for horses, since the stud of a single satrap consisted of 800 stallions and 16,000 mares.

Susianian horses (Koyunjik).

If we may judge of the character of Babylonian from that of Susianian steeds, we may consider the breed to have, been strong and large limbed, but not very handsome, the head being too large and the legs too short for beauty.

The Babylonians were also from very early times famous for their breed of dogs. The tablet engraved in a former volume, which gives a representation of a Babylonian hound, is probably of a high antiquity, not later than the period or the Empire.

Babylonian dog from a gem.

Dogs are also not unfrequently represented on ancient Babylonian stones and cylinders. It would seem that, as in Assyria, there were two principal breeds, one somewhat clumsy and heavy, of a character not unlike that of our mastiff, the other of a much lighter make, nearly resembling our greyhound. The former kind is probably the breed known as Indian, which was kept up by continual importations from the country whence it was originally derived.

We have no evidence that camels were employed in the time of the Empire, either by the Babylonians themselves or by their neighbors, the Susianians; but in Upper Mesopotamia, in Syria, and in Palestine they had been in use from a very early date. The Amalekitos and the Midianites found them serviceable in war; and the latter people employed them also as beasts of burden in their caravan trade. The Syrians of Upper Mesopotamia rode upon them in their journeys. It appears that they were also sometimes yoked to chariots, though from their size and clumsiness they would be but ill fitted for beasts of draught.

Buffaloes were, it is probable, domesticated by the Babylonians at an early date. The animal seems to have been indigenous in the country, and it is far better suited for the marshy regions of Lower Babylonia and Susiana than cattle of the ordinary kind. It is perhaps a buffalo which is represented on an ancient tablet already referred to, where a lion is disturbed in the middle of his feast off a prostrate animal by a man armed with a hatchet. Cows and oxen, however, of the common kind are occasionally represented on the cylinders, where they seem sometimes to represent animals about to be offered to the gods. Goats also appear frequently in this capacity; and they were probably more common than sheep, at any rate in the more southern districts.

Of Babylonian sheep we have no representations at all on the monuments; but it is scarcely likely that a country which used wool so largely was content to be without them. At any rate they abounded in the provinces, forming the chief wealth of the more northern nations.

Oxen, from Babylonian Cylinders.

Chapter III. The People

"The Chaldaeans, that bitter and hasty nation."—Habak. 1. 6.

The Babylonians, who, under Nabopolassar and Nebuchadnezzar, held the second place among the nations of the East, were emphatically a mixed race. The ancient people from whom they were in the main descended-the Chaldaeans of the First Empire-possessed this character to a considerable extent, since they united Cusbite with Turanian blood, and contained moreover a slight Semitic and probably a slight Arian element. But the Babylonians of later times-the Chaldaeans of the Hebrew prophets-must have been very much more a mixed race than their earlier namesakes-partly in consequence of the policy of colonization pursued systematically by the later Assyrian kings, partly from the direct influence exerted upon them by conquerors. Whatever may have been the case with the Arab dynasty, which bore sway in the country from about B.C. 1546 till B.C. 1300, it is certain that the Assyrians conquered Babylon about B.C. 1300, and almost certain that they established an Assyrian family upon the throne of Nimrod, which held for some considerable time the actual sovereignty of the country. It was natural that under a dynasty of Semites, Semitic blood should flow freely into the lower region, Semitic usages and modes of thought become prevalent, and the spoken language of the country pass from a Turanian or Turano-Cushite to a Semitic type. The previous Chaldaean race blended, apparently, with the new comers, and people was produced in which the three elements-the Semitic, the Turanian, and the Cushite-held about equal shares. The colonization of the Sargonid kings added probably other elements in small proportions, and the result was that among all the nations inhabiting Western Asia there can have been none so thoroughly deserving the title of a "mingled people" as the Babylonians of the later Empire.

In mixtures of this kind it is almost always found that some one element practically preponderates, and assumes to itself the right of fashioning and forming the general character of the race. It is not at all necessary that this formative element should be larger than any other; on the contrary, it may be and sometimes is extremely small; for it does not work by its mass, but by its innate force and strong vital energy. In Babylonia, the element which showed itself to possess this superior vitality, which practically asserted its pre-eminence and proceeded to mold the national character, was the Semitic. There is abundant evidence that by the time of the later Empire the Babylonians had become thoroughly Semitized; so much so, that ordinary observers scarcely distinguished them from their purely Semitic neighbors, the Assyrians. No doubt there were differences which a Hippocrates or an Aristotle could have detected-differences resulting from mixed descent, as well as differences arising from climate and physical geography; but, speaking broadly, it must be said that the Semitic element, introduced into Babylonia from the north, had so prevailed by the time of the establishment of the Empire that the race was no longer one sui generis, but was a mere variety of the well-known and widely spread Semitic type.

We possess but few notices, and fewer assured representations, from which to form an opinion of the physical characteristics of the Babylonians. Except upon the cylinders, there are extant only three or four representations of the human forms by Babylonian artists, and in the few cases where this form occurs we cannot always feel at all certain that the intention is to portray a human being. A few Assyrian bas-reliefs probably represent campaigns in Babylonia; but the Assyrians vary their human type so little that these sculptures must not be regarded as conveying to us very exact information. Tho cylinders are too rudely executed to be of much service, and they seem to preserve an archaic type which originated with the Proto-Chaldaeans. If we might trust the figures upon them as at all nearly representing the truth, we should have to regard the Babylonians as of much slighter and sparer frames than their northern neighbors, of a physique in fact approaching to meagreness. The Assyrian sculptures, however, are far from bearing out this idea; from them it would seem that the frames of the Babylonians were as brawny and massive as those of the Assyrians themselves, while in feature there was not much difference between the nations. Foreheads straight but not high, noses well formed but somewhat depressed, full lips, and a well-marked rounded chin, constitute the physiognomy of the Babylonians as it appears upon the sculptures of their neighbors.

Babylonian men,
from the Assyrian sculptures.

This representation is not contradicted by the few specimens of actual sculpture left by themselves. In these the type approaches nearly to the Assyrian, while there is still, such an amount of difference as renders it tolerably easy to distinguish between the productions of the two nations. The eye is larger, and not so decidedly almond-shaped; the nose is shorter, and its depression is still more marked; while the general expression of the countenance is altogether more commonplace.

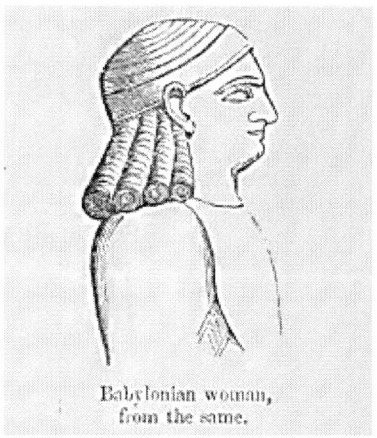

Babylonian woman,
from the same.

These differences may be probably referred to the influence which was exercised upon the physical form of the race by the primitive or Proto-Chaldaean element, an influence which appears to have been considerable. This element, as has been already observed, was predominantly Cushite; and there is reason to believe that the Cushite race was connected not very remotely with the negro. In Susiana, where the Cushite blood was maintained in tolerable purity-Elymseans and Kissians existing side by side, instead of blending together-there was, if we may trust the Assyrian remains, a very decided prevalency of a negro type of countenance, as the accompanying specimens, carefully copied from the sculptures, will render evident.

Susianians (Koyunjik).

The head was covered with short crisp curls; the eye was large, the nose and mouth nearly in the same line, the lips thick. Such a physiognomy as the Babylonian appears to have been would naturally arise from an intermixture of a race like the Assyrian with one resembling that which the later sculptures represent as the main race inhabiting Susiana.

Heads of Babylonians, from the Cylinders.

Head of an Elamitic chief
(Koyunjik).

Herodotus remarks that the Babylonians wore their hair long; and this remark is confirmed to some extent by the native remains. These in general represent the hair as forming a single stiff and heavy curl at the back of the head (No. 3). Sometimes, however, they make it take the shape of long flowing locks, which depend over the back (No. 1), or over the back and shoulders (No. 4), reaching nearly to the waist. Occasionally, in lieu of these commoner types, we have one which closely resembles the Assyrian, the hair forming a round mass behind the head (No. 2), on which we can sometimes trace indications of a slight wave. The national fashion, that to which Herodotus alludes, seems to be represented by the three commoner modes. Where the round mass is worn, we have probably an Assyrian fashion, which the Babylonians aped during the time of that people's pre-eminence.

Heads of Babylonians,
from the Cylinders.

Head of an Elamitic chief
(Koyunjik).

Besides their flowing hair, the Babylonians are represented frequently with a large beard. This is generally longer than the Assyrian, descending nearly to the waist. Sometimes it curls crisply upon the face, but below the chin depends over the breast in long, straight locks. At other times it droops perpendicularly from the cheeks and the under lip.15 Frequently, however, the beard is shaven off, and the whole face is smooth and hairless.

The Chaldaean females, as represented by the Assyrians, are tall and large-limbed. Their physiognomy is Assyrian, their hair not very abundant. The Babylonian cylinders, on the other hand, make the hair long and conspicuous, while the forms are quite as spare and meagre as those of the men.

On the whole, it is most probable that the physical type of the later Babylonians was nearly that of their northern neighbors. A somewhat sparer form, longer and more flowing hair, and features less stern and strong, may perhaps have characterized them. They were also, it is probable, of a darker complexion than the Assyrians, being to some extent Ethiopians by descent, and inhabiting a region which lies four degrees nearer to the tropics than Assyria. The Cha'ab Arabs, the present possessors of the more southern parts of Babylonia, are nearly black; and the "black Syrians," of whom Strabo speaks, seem intended to represent the Babylonians.

Among the moral and mental characteristics of the people, the first place is due to their intellectual ability. Inheriting a legacy of scientific knowledge, astronomical and arithmetical, from the Proto-Chaldaeans, they seem to have not only maintained but considerably advanced these sciences by their own efforts. Their "wisdom and learning" are celebrated by the Jewish prophets Isaiah, Jeremiah, and Daniel; the Father of History records their valuable inventions; and an Aristotle was not ashamed to be beholden to them for scientific data. They were good observers of astronomical phenomena, careful recorders of such observations, and mathematicians of no small repute. Unfortunately, they mixed with their really scientific studies those occult pursuits which, in ages and countries where the limits of true science are not known, are always apt to seduce students from the right path, having attractions against which few men are proof, so long as it is believed that they can really accomplish the end that they propose to themselves. The Babylonians were astrologers no less than astronomers; they professed to cast nativities, to expound dreams, and to foretell events by means of the stars; and though there were always a certain number who kept within the legitimate bounds of science, and repudiated the astrological pretensions of their brethren, yet on the whole it must be allowed that their astronomy was fatally tinged with a mystic and unscientific element.

In close connection with the intellectual ability of the Babylonians was the spirit of enterprise which led them to engage in traffic and to adventure themselves upon the ocean in ships. In a future chapter we shall have to consider the extent and probable direction of this commerce. It is sufficient to observe in the present place that the same turn of mind which made the Phoenicians anciently the great carriers between the East and West, and which in modern times has rendered the Jews so successful in various branches of trade, seems to have characterized the Semitized Babylonians, whose land was emphatically "a land of traffic," and their chief city "a city of merchants."

The trading spirit which was thus strongly developed in the Babylonian people led naturally to the two somewhat opposite vices of avarice and over-luxuriousness. Not content with honorable gains, the Babylonians "coveted an evil covetousness," as we learn both from Habakkuk and Jeremiah. The "shameful custom" mentioned by Herodotus, which required as a religious duty that every Babylonian woman, rich or poor, highborn or humble, should once in her life prostitute herself in the temple of Beltis, was probably based on the desire of attracting strangers to the capital, who would either bring with them valuable commodities or purchase the productions of the country. The public auction of marriageable virgins had most likely a similar intention. If we may believe Curtius, strangers might at any time purchase the gratification of any passion they might feel, from the avarice of parents or husbands.

The luxury of the Babylonians is a constant theme with both sacred and profane writers. The "daughter of the Chaldaeans" was "tender and delicate," "given to pleasures," apt to "dwell carelessly." Her young men made themselves "as princes to look at-exceeding in dyed attire upon their heads," —painting their faces, wearing earrings, and clothing themselves in robes of soft and rich material. Extensive polygamy prevailed. The pleasures of the table were carried to excess. Drunkenness was common. Rich unguents were invented. The tables groaned under the weight of gold and silver plate. In every possible way the Babylonians practised luxuriousness of living, and in respect of softness and self-indulgence they certainly did not fall short of any nation of antiquity.

There was, however, a harder and sterner side to the Babylonian character. Despite their love of luxury, they were at all times brave and skilful in war; and, during the period of their greatest strength, they were one of the most formidable of all the nations of the East. Habakkuk describes them, drawing evidently from the life, as "bitter and hasty," and again as "terrible and dreadful-their horses' hoofs swifter than the leopard's, and more fierce than the evening wolves." Hence they "smote the people in wrath with a continual stroke" —they "made the earth to tremble, and did shake kingdoms" —they carried all before them in their great enterprises, seldom allowing themselves to be foiled by resistance, or turned from their course by pity. Exercised for centuries in long and fierce wars with the well-armed and well-disciplined Assyrians, they were no sooner quit of this enemy, and able to take an aggressive attitude, than they showed themselves no unworthy successors of that long-dominant nation, so far as energy, valor, and military skill constitute desert. They carried their victorious arms from the shores of the Persian Gulf to the banks of the Nile; wherever they went, they rapidly established their power, crushing all resistance, and fully meriting the remarkable title, which they seem to have received from those who had felt their attacks, of "the hammer of the whole earth."

The military successes of the Babylonians were accompanied with needless violence, and with outrages not unusual in the East, which the historian must nevertheless regard as at once crimes and follies. The transplantation of conquered races —a part of the policy of Assyria which the Chaldaeans adopted-may perhaps have been morally defensible, notwithstanding the sufferings which it involved. But the mutilations of prisoners, the weary imprisonments, the massacre of non-combatants, the refinement of cruelty shown in the execution of children before the eyes of their fathers-these and similar atrocities, which are recorded of the Babylonians, are wholly without excuse, since they did not so much terrify as exasperate the conquered nations, and thus rather endangered than added strength or security to the empire. A savage and inhuman temper is betrayed by these harsh punishments —a temper common in Asiatics, but none the less reprehensible on that account-one that led its possessors to sacrifice interest to vengeance, and the peace of a kingdom to a tiger-like thirst for blood. Nor was this cruel temper shown only towards the subject nations and captives taken in war. Babylonian nobles trembled for their heads if they incurred by a slight fault the displeasure of the monarch; and even the most powerful class in the kingdom, the learned and venerable "Chaldaeans," ran on one occasion the risk of being exterminated, because they could not expound a dream which the king had forgotten. If a monarch displeased his court, and was regarded as having a bad disposition, it was not thought enough simply to make away with him, but he was put to death by torture. Among recognized punishments were cutting to pieces and casting into a heated furnace. The houses of offenders were pulled down and made into dunghills. These practices imply a "violence" and cruelty beyond the ordinary Oriental limit; and we cannot be surprised that when final judgment was denounced against Babylon, it was declared to be sent, in a great measure, "because of men's blood, and for the violence of the land-of the city, and all that dwelt therein."

It is scarcely necessary to add that the Babylonians were a proud people. Pride is unfortunately the invariable accompaniment of success, in the nation, if not in the individual; and the sudden elevation of Babylon from a subject to a dominant power must have been peculiarly trying, more especially to the Oriental temperament. The spirit which culminated in Nebuchadnezzar, when, walking in the palace of his kingdom, and surveying the magnificent buildings which he had raided on every side from the plunder of the conquered nations, and by the labor of their captive bands, he exclaimed, "Is not the great Babylon which I have built by the might of my power and for the honor of my majesty?" —was rife in the people generally, who, naturally enough, believed themselves superior to every other nation upon the earth. "I am, and there is none else beside me," was the thought, if not the speech, of the people, whose arrogancy was perhaps somewhat less offensive than that of the Assyrians, but was quite as intense and as deep-seated.

The Babylonians, notwithstanding their pride, their cruelty, their covetousness, and their love of luxury, must be pronounced to have been, according to their lights, a religious people. The temple in Babylonia is not a mere adjunct of the palace, but has almost the same pre-eminence over other buildings which it claims in Egypt. The vast mass of the Birs-i-Nimrud is sufficient to show that an enormous amount of labor was expended in the erection of sacred edifices; and the costly ornamentation lavished on such buildings is, as we shall hereafter find, even more remarkable than their size. Vast sums wore also expended on images of the gods, necessary adjuncts of the religion; and the whole paraphernalia of worship exhibited a rare splendor and magnificence. The monarchs were devout worshippers of the various deities, and gave much of their attention to the building and repair of temples, the erection of images, and the like. They bestowed on their children names indicative of religious feeling, and implying real faith in the power of the gods to protect their votaries. The people generally affected similar names-names containing, in almost every case, a god's name as one of their elements. The seals or signets which formed almost a necessary part of each man's costume were, except in rare instances, of a religious character. Even in banquets, where we might have expected that thoughts of religion would be laid aside, it seems to have been the practice during the drinking to rehearse the praises of the deities.

We are told by Nicolas of Damascus that the Babylonians cultivated two virtues especially, honesty and calmness. Honesty is the natural, almost the necessary virtue of traders, who soon find that it is the best policy to be fair and just in their dealings. We may well believe that this intelligent people had the wisdom to see their true interests, and to understand that trade can never prosper unless conducted with integrity and straightforwardness. The very fact that their trade did prosper, that their goods were everywhere in request, is sufficient proof of their commercial honesty, and of their superiority to those tricks which speedily ruin a commerce.

Calmness is not a common Oriental virtue. It is not even in general very highly appreciated, being apt to strike the lively, sensitive, and passionate Eastern as mere dulness and apathy. In China, however, it is a point of honor that the outward demeanor should be calm and placid under any amount of provocation; and indignation, fierceness, even haste, are regarded as signs of incomplete civilization, which the disciples of Confucius love to note in their would-be rivals of the West.

We may conceive that some similar notion was entertained by the proud Babylonians, who no doubt regarded themselves as infinitely superior in manners and culture, no less than in scientific attainments, to the "barbarians" of Persia and Greece. While rage boiled in their hearts, and commands to torture and destroy fell from their tongues, etiquette may have required that the countenance should be unmoved, the eye serene, the voice low and gentle. Such contrasts are not uncommonly seen in the polite Mandarin, whose apparent calmness drives his European antagonist to despair; and it may well be that the Babylonians of the sixth and seventh centuries before our era had attained to an equal power of restraining the expression of feeling. But real gentleness, meekness, and placability were certainly not the attributes of a people who were so fierce in their wars and so cruel in their punishments.

Chapter IV. The Capital

Πόλισμα ονομαστοτατον και ισχυρότατόν. — Herod, i. 178.

Babylon, the capital of the Fourth Monarchy, was probably the largest and most magnificent city of the ancient world. A dim tradition current in the East gave, it is true, a greater extent, if not a greater splendor, to the metropolis of Assyria; but this tradition first appears in ages subsequent to the complete destruction of the more northern city; and it is contradicted by the testimony of facts. The walls of Nineveh have been completely traced, and indicate a city three miles in length, by less than a mile and a half in breadth, containing an area of about 1800 English acres. Of this area less than one tenth is occupied by ruins of any pretension. On the admitted site of Babylon striking masses of ruin cover a space considerably larger than that which at Nineveh constitutes the whole area of the town. Beyond this space in every direction, north, east, south and west, are detached mounds indicating the former existence of edifices of some size, while the intermediate ground between these mounds and the main ruins shows distinct traces of its having been built upon in former days.

Of the actual size of the town, modern research gives us no clear and definite notion. One explorer only has come away from the country with an idea that the general position of the detached mounds, by which the plain around Hillah is dotted, enables him to draw the lines of the ancient walls, and mark out the exact position of the city. But the very maps and plans which are put forward in support of this view show that it rests mainly on hypothesis; nor is complete confidence placed in the surveys on which the maps and plans have been constructed. The English surveys, which have been unfortunately lost, are said not to have placed the detached mounds in any such decided lines as M. Oppert believes them to occupy, and the general impression of the British officers who were employed on the service is that "no vestige of the walls of Babylon has been as yet discovered."

For the size and plan of the city we are thus of necessity thrown back upon the reports of ancient authors. It is not pretended that such reports are in this, or in any other case, deserving of implicit credence. The ancient historians, even the more trustworthy of them, are in the habit of exaggerating in their numbers; and on such subjects as measurements they were apt to take on trust the declarations of their native guides, who would be sure to make over-statements. Still in this instance we have so many distinct authorities-eyewitnesses of the facts-and some of them belonging to times when scientific accuracy had begun to be appreciated, that we must be very in credulous if we do not accept their witness, so far as it is consentient, and not intrinsically very improbable.

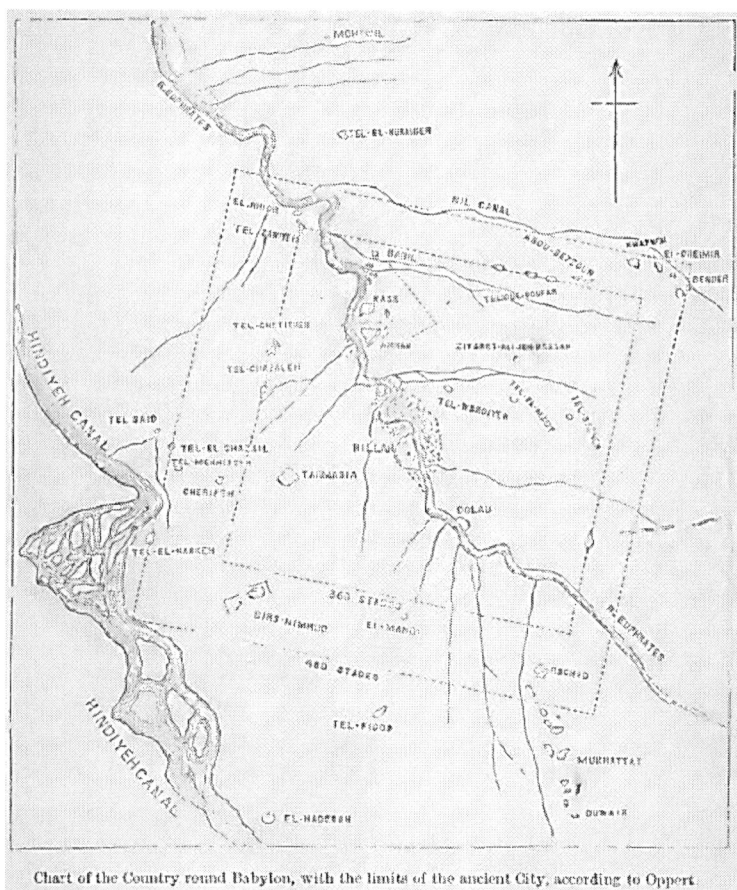

Chart of the Country round Babylon, with the limits of the ancient City, according to Oppert.

According to Herodotus, an eye-witness, and the earliest authority on the subject the *enceinte* of Babylon was a square, 120 stades (about 14 miles) each way-the entire circuit of the wall being thus 56 miles, and the area enclosed within them falling little short of 200 square miles. Ctesias, also an eyewitness, and the next writer on the subject, reduced the circuit of the walls to 360 stades, or 41 miles, and made the area consequently little more than 100 square miles. These two estimates are respectively the greatest and the least that have come down to us. The historians of Alexander, while conforming nearly to the statements of Ctesias, a little enlarge his dimensions, making the circuit 365, 368, or 385 stades. The differences here are inconsiderable; and it seems to be established, on a weight of testimony which we rarely possess in such a matter, that the walls of this great town were about forty miles in circumference, and enclosed an area as large as that of the Landgraviat of Hesse-Homburg.

It is difficult to suppose that the real city-the streets and squares-can at any time have occupied one half of this enormous area, A clear space, we are told, was left for a considerable distance inside the wall-like the *pomaerium* of the Romans-upon which no houses were allowed to be built. When houses began, they were far from being continuous; gardens, orchards, even fields, were interspersed among the buildings; and it was supposed that the inhabitants, when besieged, could grow sufficient corn for their own consumption within the walls. Still the whole area was laid out with straight streets, or perhaps one should say with roads (for the houses cannot have been continuous along them), which cut one another everywhere at right angles, like the streets of some German towns. The wall of the town was pierced with a hundred gates, twenty-five (we may suppose) in each face, and the roads led straight to these portals, the whole area being thus cut up into square blocks. The houses were in general lofty, being three or even four stories high. They are said to have had vaulted roofs, which were not protected externally with any tiling, since the climate was so dry as to render such a protection unnecessary. The beams used in the houses were of palm-wood, all other timber being scarce in the country; and such pillars as the houses could boast were of the same material. The construction of these last was very rude. Around posts of palm-wood were twisted wisps of rushes, which were covered with plaster, and then colored according the taste of the owner.

The Euphrates ran through the town, dividing it nearly in half. Its banks were lined throughout with quays of brick laid in bitumen, and were further guarded by two walls of brick, which skirted them along their whole length. In each of these walls were twenty-five gates, corresponding to the number of the streets which gave upon the river; and outside each gate was a sloped landing place, by which you could descend to the water's edge, if you had occasion to cross the river. Boats were kept ready at these landing-places to convey passengers from side to side; while for those who disliked this method of conveyance a bridge was provided of a somewhat peculiar construction. A number of stone piers were erected in the bed of the stream, firmly clamped together with fastenings of iron and lead; wooden drawbridges connected pier with pier during the day, and on these passengers passed over; but at night they were withdrawn, in order that the bridge might not be used during the dark. Diodorus declares that besides this bridge, to which he assigns a length of five stades (about 1000 yards) and a breadth of 30 feet, the two sides of the river were joined together by a tunnel, which was fifteen feet wide and twelve high to the spring of its arched roof.

The most remarkable buildings which the city contained were the two palaces, one on either side of the river, and the great temple of Belus. Herodotus describes the great temple as contained within a square enclosure, two stades (nearly a quarter of a mile) both in length and breadth. Its chief feature was the *ziggurat* or tower, a huge solid mass of brick-work, built (like all Babylonian temple-towers) in stages, square being emplaced on square, and a sort of rude pyramid being thus formed, at the top of which was the main shrine of the god. The basement platform of the Belus tower was, Herodotus tells us, a stade, or rather more than 200 yards, each way. The number of stages was eight. The ascent to the highest stage, which contained the shrine of the god, was on the outside, and consisted either of steps, or of an inclined plane, carried round the four sides of the building, and in this way conducting to the top. According to Strabo the tower was a stado (606 feet 9 inches) in height; but this estimate, if it is anything more than a conjecture, must represent rather the length of the winding ascent than the real altitude of the building. The great pyramid itself was only 480 feet high; and it is very questionable whether any Babylonian building ever equalled it. About half-way up the ascent was a resting-place with seats, where persons commonly sat a while on their way to the summit. The shrine which crowned the edifice was large and rich. In the time of Herodotus it contained no image; but only a golden table and a large couch, covered with a handsome drapery. This, however, was after the Persian conquest and the plunder of its principal treasures. Previously, if we may believe Diodorus, the shrine was occupied by three colossal images of gold-one of Bel, one of Beltis, and the third of Rhea or Ishtar. Before the image of Beltis were two golden lions, and near them two enormous serpents of silver, each thirty talents in weight. The golden table-forty feet long and fifteen broad-was in front of these statues, and upon it stood two huge drinking-cups, of the same weight as the serpents. The shrine also contained two enormous censers and three golden bowls, one for each of the three deities.

At the base of the tower was a second shrine or chapel, which in the time of Herodotus contained a sitting image of Bel, made of gold, with a golden table in front of it, and a stand for the image, of the same precious metal. Here, too, Persian avarice had been busy; for anciently this shrine had possessed a second statue, which was a human figure twelve cubits high, made of solid gold. The shrine was also rich in private offerings. Outside the building, but within the sacred enclosure, were two altars, a smaller one of gold, on which it was customary to offer sucklings, and a larger one, probably of stone, where the worshippers sacrificed full-grown victims.

The great palace was a building of still larger dimensions than the great temple. According to Diodorus, it was situated within a triple enclosure, the innermost wall being twenty stades, the second forty stades, and the outermost sixty stades (nearly seven miles), in circumference. The outer wall was built entirely of plain baked brick. The middle and inner walls were of the same material, fronted with enamelled bricks representing hunting scenes. The figures, according to this author, were larger than the life, and consisted chiefly of a great variety of animal forms. There were not wanting, however, a certain number of human forms to enliven the scene; and among these were two —a man thrusting his spear through a lion, and a woman on horseback aiming at a leopard with her javelin-which the later Greeks believed to represent the mythic Ninus and Semiramis. Of the character of the apartments we hear nothing; but we are told that the palace had three gates, two of which were of bronze, and that these had to be opened and shut by a machine.

But the main glory of the palace was its pleasure-ground —the "Hanging Gardens," which the Greeks regarded as one of the seven wonders of the world. This extraordinary construction, which owed its erection to the whim of a woman, was a square, each side of which measured 400 Greek feet. It was supported upon several tiers of open arches, built one over the other, like the walls of a classic theatre, and sustaining at each stage, or story, a solid platform, from which the piers of the next tier of arches rose. The building towered into the air to the height of at least seventy-five feet, and was covered at the top with a great mass of earth, in which there grew not merely flowers and shrubs, but tress also of the largest size. Water was supplied from the Euphrates through pipes, and was raised (it is said) by a screw, working on the principal of Archimedes. To prevent the moisture from penetrating into the brick-work and gradually destroying the building, there were interposed between the bricks and the mass of soil, first a layer of reeds mixed with bitumen, then a double layer of burnt brick cemented with gypsum, and thirdly a coating of sheet lead. The ascent to the garden was by steps. On the way up, among the arches which sustained the building, were stately apartments, which, must have been pleasant from their coolness. There was also a chamber within the structure containing the machinery by which the water was raised.

Of the smaller palace, which was opposite to the larger one, on the other side the river, but few details have come down to us. Like the larger palace, it was guarded by a triple enclosure, the entire circuit of which measured (it is said) thirty stades. It contained a number of bronze statues, which the Greeks believed to represent the god Belus, and the sovereigns Ninus and Semiramis, together with their officers. The walls were covered with battle scenes and hunting scenes, vividly represented by means of bricks painted and enamelled.

Such was the general character of the town and its chief edifices, if we may believe the descriptions of eye-witnesses. The walls which enclosed and guarded the whole-or which, perhaps one should rather say, guarded the district within which Babylon was placed-have been already mentioned as remarkable for their great extent, but cannot be dismissed without a more special and minute description. Like the "Hanging Gardens," they were included among the "world's seven wonders," and, according to every account given of them, their magnitude and construction were remarkable.

It has been already noticed that, according to the lowest of the ancient estimates, the entire length of the walls was 360 stades, or more than forty-one miles. With respect to the width we have two very different statements, one by Herodotus and the other by Clitarchus and Strabo. Herodotus makes the width 50 royal cubits, or about 85 English feet, Strabo and Q. Curtius reduced the estimate to 32 feet. There is still greater discrepancy with respect to the height of the walls. Herodotus says that the height was 200 royal cubits, or 300 royal feet (about 335 English feet); Ctesias made it 50 fathoms, or 300 ordinary Greek feet; Pliny and Solinus, substituting feet for the royal cubits of Herodotus, made the altitude 235 feet; Philostratus and Q. Curtius, following perhaps some one of Alexander's historians, gave for the height 150 feet; finally Clitarchus, as reported by Diodorus Siculus, and Strabo, who probably followed him, have left us the very moderate estimate of 75 feet. It is impossible to reconcile these numbers. The supposition that some of them belong properly to the outer, and others to the inner wall, will not explain the discrepancies-for the measurements cannot by any ingenuity be reduced to two sets of dimensions. The only conclusion which it seems possible to draw from the conflicting testimony is that the numbers were either rough guesses made by very unskilful travellers, or else were (in most cases) intentional exaggerations palmed upon them by the native ciceroni. Still the broad facts remain-first, that the walls enclosed an enormous space, which was very partially occupied by buildings; secondly, that they were of great and unusual thickness; and thirdly, that they were of a vast height-seventy or eighty feet at least in the time of Alexander, after the wear and tear of centuries and the violence of at least three conquerors.

The general character of the construction is open to but little doubt. The wall was made of bricks, either baked in kilns, or (more probably) dried in the sun, and laid in a cement of bitumen, with occasional layers of reeds between the courses. Externally it was protected by a wide and deep moat. On the summit were low towers, rising above the wall to the height of some ten or fifteen feet, and probably serving as guardrooms for the defenders. These towers are said to have been 250 in number; they were least numerous on the western face of the city, where the wall ran along the marshes. They were probably angular, not round; and instead of extending through the whole thickness of the wall, they were placed along its outer and inner edge, tower facing tower, with a wide space between them —"enough," Herodotus says, "for a four-horse chariot to turn in." The wall did not depend on them for its strength, but on its own height and thickness, which were such as to render scaling and mining equally hopeless.

Such was Babylon, according to the descriptions of the ancients —a great city, built on a very regular plan, surrounded by populous suburbs interspersed among fields and gardens, the whole being included within a large square strongly fortified enceinte. When we turn from this picture of the past to contemplate the present condition of the localities, we are at first struck with astonishment at the small traces which remain of so vast and wonderful a metropolis. "The broad walls of Babylon" are "utterly broken" down, and her "high gates burned with fire." "The golden city hath ceased." God has "swept it with the bosom of destruction." "The glory of the kingdoms, the beauty of the Chaldees' excellency," is become "as when God overthrew Sodom and Gomorrha." The traveller who passes through the land is at first inclined to say that there are no ruins, no remains, of the mighty city which once lorded it over the earth. By and by, however, he begins to see that though ruins, in the common acceptation of the term, scarcely exist-though there are no arches, no pillars, but one or two appearances of masonry even yet the whole country is covered with traces of exactly that kind which it was prophesied Babylon should leave. Vast "heaps" or mounds, shapeless and unsightly, are scattered at intervals over the entire region where it is certain that Babylon anciently stood, and between the "heaps" the soil is in many places composed of fragments of pottery and bricks, and deeply impregnated with nitre, infallible indications of its having once been covered with buildings. As the traveller descends southward from Baghdad he finds these indications increase, until, on nearing the Euphrates, a few miles beyond Mohawil, he notes that they have become continuous, and finds himself in a region of mounds, some of which are of enormous size.

These mounds begin about five miles above Hillah, and extend for a distance of about three miles from north to south along the course of the river, lying principally on its left or eastern bank. The ruins on this side consist chiefly of three great masses of building. The most northern, to which the Arabs of the present day apply the name of BABIL-the true native appellation of the ancient citys-is a vast pile of brick-work of an irregular quadrilateral shape, with precipitous sides furrowed by ravines, and with a flat top. Of the four faces of the ruin the southern seems to be the most perfect. It extends a distance of about 200 yards, or almost exactly a stade, and runs nearly in a straight line from west to east. At its eastern extremity it forms a right angle with the east face, which runs nearly due north for about 180 yards, also almost in a straight line. The western and northern faces are apparently much worn away. Here are the chief ravines, and here is the greatest seeming deviation from the original lines of the building. The greatest height of the Babil mound is 130 or 140 feet. It is mainly composed of sun-dried brick, but shows signs of having been faced with fire-burnt brick, carefully cemented with an excellent white mortar. The bricks of this outer facing bear the name and titles of Nebuchadnezzar. A very small portion of the original structure has been laid bare enough however to show that the lines of the building did not slope like those of a pyramid, but were perpendicular, and that the side walls had, at intervals, the support of buttresses.

View of the Babil mound from the Kasr.

This vast building, whatever it was, stood within a square enclosure, two sides of which, the northern and eastern, are still very distinctly marked. A long low line of rampart runs for 400 yards parallel to the east face of the building, at a distance of 120 or 130 yards, and a similar but somewhat longer line of mound runs parallel to the north face at rather a greater distance from it. On the west a third line could be traced in the early part of the present century; but it appears to be now obliterated. Here and on the south are the remains of an ancient canal, the construction of which may have caused the disappearance of the southern, and of the lower part of the western line.

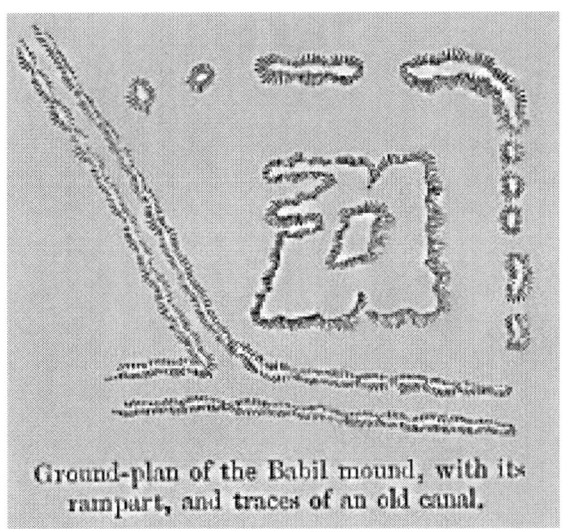

Ground-plan of the Babil mound, with its rampart, and traces of an old canal.

Below the Babil mound, which stands isolated from the rest of the ruins, are two principal masses-the more northern known to the Arabs as EL KASR, "the Palace," and the more southern as "the mound of Amran," from the tomb of a reputed prophet Amran-ibn-Ali, which crowns its summit. The Kasr mound is an oblong square, about 700 yards long by 600 broad, with the sides facing the cardinal points. Its height above the plain is 70 feet. Its longer direction is from north to south.

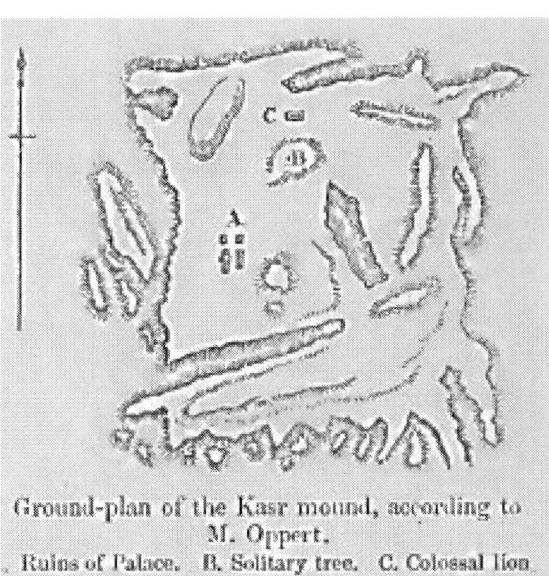

Ground-plan of the Kasr mound, according to M. Oppert.
Ruins of Palace. B. Solitary tree. C. Colossal lion

As far as it has been penetrated, it consists mainly of rubbish-loose bricks, tiles, and fragments of stone. In a few places only are there undisturbed remains of building. One such relic is a subterranean passage, seven feet in height, floored and walled with baked brick, and covered in at the top with great blocks of sandstone, which may either have been a secret exit or more probably an enormous drain. Another is the Kasr, or "palace" proper, whence the mound has its name. This is a fragment of excellent brick masonry in a wonderful state of preservation, consisting of walls, piers, and buttresses, and in places ornamented with pilasters, but of too fragmentary a character to furnish the modern inquirer with any clue to the original plan of the building. The bricks are of a pale yellow color and of the best possible quality, nearly resembling our fire-bricks. They are stamped, one and all, with the name and titles of Nebuchadnezzar. The mortar in which they are laid is a fine lime cement, which adheres so closely to the bricks that it is difficult to obtain a specimen entire. In the dust at the foot of the walls are numerous fragments of brick, painted, and covered with a thick enamel or glaze. Here, too, have been found a few fragments of sculptured stone, and slabs containing an account of the erection of a palatial edifice by Nebuchadnezzar. Near the northern edge of the mound, and about midway in its breadth, is a colossal figure of a lion, rudely carved in black basalt, standing over the prostrate figure of a man with arms outstretched. A single tree grows on the huge ruin, which the Arabs declare to be of a species not known elsewhere, and regard as a remnant of the hanging garden of Bokht-i-nazar. It is a tamarisk of no rare kind, but of very great ago, in consequence of which, and of its exposed position, the growth and foliage are somewhat peculiar.

South of the Kasr mound, at the distance of about 800 yards, is the remaining great mass of ruins, the mound of Jumjuma, or of Amran. The general shape of this mound is triangular,107 but it is very irregular and ill-defined, so as scarcely to admit of accurate description. Its three sides face respectively a little east of north, a little south of east, and a little south of west. The south-western side, which runs nearly parallel with the Euphrates, and seems to have been once washed by the river, is longer than either of the others, extending a distance of above a thousand yards, while the south-eastern may be 800 yards, and the north-eastern 700. Innumerable ravines traverse the mound on every side, penetrating it nearly to its centre.

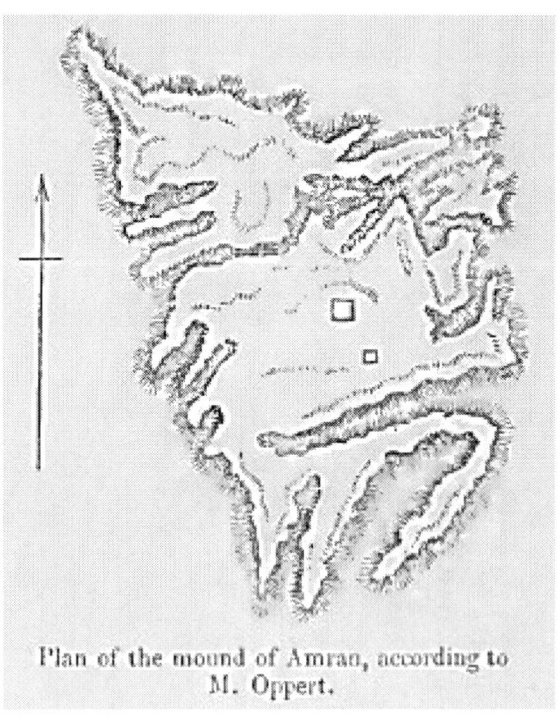

Plan of the mound of Amran, according to M. Oppert.

The surface is a series of undulations. Neither masonry nor sculpture is anywhere apparent.
All that meets the eye is a mass of debris; and the researches hitherto made have failed to bring to light any distinct traces of building. Occasionally bricks are found, generally of poor material, and bearing the names and titles of some of the earlier Babylonian monarchs; but the trenches opened in the pile have in no case laid bare even the smallest fragment of a wall.

Besides the remains which have been already described, the most remarkable are certain long lines of rampart on both sides of the river, which lie outside of the other ruins, enclosing them all, except the mound of Babil. On the left bank of the stream there is to be traced, in the first place, a double line of wall or rampart, having a direction nearly due north and south, which lies east of the Kasr and Amran mounds, at the distance from them of about 1000 yards. Beyond this is a single line of rampart to the north-east, traceable for about two miles, the direction of which is nearly from north-west to south-east, and a double line of rampart to the south-east, traceable for a mile and a half, with a direction from northeast to south-west. The two lines in this last case are from 600 to 700 yards apart, and diverge from one another as they run out to the north-east. The inner of the two meets the north-eastern rampart nearly at a right angle, and is clearly a part of the same work. It is questioned, however, whether this line of fortification is ancient, and not rather a construction belonging to Parthian times.

A low line of mounds is traceable between the western face of the Amran and Kasr hills, and the present eastern bank of the river, bounding a sort of narrow valley, in which either the main stream of the Euphrates, or at any rate a branch from it, seems anciently to have flowed.

General Chart of the Ruins of Babylon.

On the right bank of the stream the chief remains are of the same kind. West of the river, a rampart, twenty feet high, runs for nearly a mile parallel with the general line of the Amran mound, at the distance of about 1000 yards from the old course of the stream. At either extremity the line of the rampart turns at a right angle, running down towards the river, and being traceable towards the north for 400 yards and towards the south for fifty or sixty. It is evident that there was once, before the stream flowed in its present channel, a rectangular enclosure, a mile long and 1000 yards broad, opposite to the Amran mound; and there are indications that within this *enceinte* was at least one important building, which was situated near the south-east angle of the enclosure, on the banks of the old course of the river. The bricks found at this point bear the name of Neriglissar.

There are also, besides the ramparts and the great masses of ruin above described, a vast number of scattered and irregular heaps of hillocks on both sides of the river, chiefly, however, upon the eastern bank. Of these one only seems to deserve distinct mention. This is the mound called El Homeira, "the Red," which lies due east of the Kasr, distant from it about 800 yards —a mound said to be 300 yards long by 100 wide, and to attain an elevation of 60 or 70 feet. It is composed of baked brick of a bright red color, and must have been a building of a very considerable height resting upon a somewhat confined base. Its bricks are inscribed along their edges, not (as is the usual practice) on their lower face.

The only other ancient work of any importance of which some remains are still to be traced is a brick embankment on the left bank of the stream between the Kasr and the Babil mounds, extending for a distance of a thousand yards in a line which has a slight curve and a general direction of S.S.W. The bricks of this embankment are of a bright red color, and of great hardness. They are laid wholly in bitumen. The legend which they bear shows that the quay was constructed by Nabonidus.

Such then are the ruins of Babylon-the whole that can now with certainty be assigned to the "beauty of the Chaldees' excellency"—the "great Babylon" of Nebuchadnezzar. Within a space little more than three miles long and a mile and three quarters broad are contained all the undoubted remains of the greatest city of the old world. These remains, however, do not serve in any way to define the ancient limits of the place. They are surrounded on every side by nitrous soil, and by low heaps which it has not been thought worth while to excavate, but which the best judges assign to the same era as the great mounds, and believe to mark the sites of the lesser temples and the other public buildings of the ancient city. Masses of this kind are most frequent to the north and east. Sometimes they are almost continuous for miles; and if we take the Kasr mound as a centre, and mark about it an area extending five miles in each direction (which would give a city of the size described by Ctesias and the historians of Alexander), we shall scarcely find a single square mile of the hundred without some indications of ancient buildings upon its surface. The case is not like that of Nineveh, where outside the walls the country is for a considerable distance singularly bare of ruins. The mass of Babylonian remains extending from Babil to Amran does not correspond to the whole *enceinte* of Nineveh, but to the mound of Koyunjik. It has every appearance of being, not the city, but "the heart of the city" —the "Royal quarter" outside of which were the streets and squares, and still further off, the vanished walls. It may seem strange that the southern capital should have so greatly exceeded the dimensions of the northern one. But, if we follow the indications presented by the respective sites, we are obliged to conclude that there was really this remarkable difference.

It has to be considered in conclusion how far we can identify the various ruins above described with the known buildings of the ancient capital, and to what extent it is possible to reconstruct upon the existing remains the true plan of the city. Fancy, if it discards the guidance of fact, may of course with the greatest ease compose plans of a charming completeness. A rigid adherence to existing data will produce, it is to be feared, a somewhat meagre and fragmentary result; but most persons will feel that this is one of the cases where the maxim of Hesiod applies — Πλέον ἥμισυ παντός —"the half is preferable to the whole:"

The one identification which may be made upon certain and indeed indisputable evidence is that of the Kasr mound with the palace built by Nebuchadnezzar. The tradition which has attached the name of Kasr or "Palace" to this heap is confirmed by inscriptions upon slabs found on the spot, wherein Nebuchadnezzar declares the building to be his "Grand Palace." The bricks of that part of the ruin which remains uncovered bear, one and all, the name of this king; and it is thus clear that here stood in ancient times the great work of which Berosus speaks as remarkable for its height and splendor. If a confirmation of the fact were needed after evidence of so decisive a character, it would be found in the correspondence between the remains found on the mound and the description left us of the "greater palace" by Diodorus. Diodorus relates that the walls of this edifice were adorned with colored representations of hunting scenes; and modern explorers find that the whole soil of the mound, and especially the part on which the fragment of ruin stands, is full of broken pieces of enamelled brick, varied in hue, and evidently containing portions of human and animal forms.

But if the Kasr represents the palace built by Nebuchadnezzar, as is generally allowed by those who have devoted their attention to the subject, it seems to follow almost as a certainty that the Amran mound is the site of that old palatial edifice to which the erection of Nebuchadnezzar was an addition. Berosus expressly states that Nebuchadnezzar's building "adjoined upon" the former palace, a description which is fairly applicable to the Amran mound by means of a certain latitude of interpretation, but which is wholly inapplicable to any of the other ruins. This argument would be conclusive, even if it stood alone. It has, however, received an important corroboration in the course of recent researches. From the Amran mound, and from this part of Babylon only, have monuments been recovered of an earlier date than Nebuchadnezzar. Here and here alone did the early kings leave memorials of their presence in Babylon; and here consequently, we may presume, stood the ancient royal residence.

If, then, all the principal ruins on the east bank of the river, with the exception of the Babil mound and the long lines marking walls or embankments, be accepted as representing the "great palace" or "citadel" of the classical writers we must recognize in the remains west of the ancient course of the river-the oblong square enclosure and the important building at its south-east angle-the second or "smaller palace" of Ctesias, which was joined to the larger one, according to that writer, by a bridge and a tunnel. This edifice, built or at any rate repaired by Neriglissar, lay directly opposite the more ancient part of the eastern palace, being separated from it by the river, which anciently flowed along the western face of the Kasr and Amran mounds. The exact position of the bridge cannot be fixed. With regard to the tunnel, it is extremely unlikely that any such construction was ever made. The "Father of History" is wholly silent on the subject, while he carefully describes the bridge, a work far less extraordinary. The tunnel rests on the authority of two writers only-Diodorus and Philostratus-who both wrote after Babylon was completely ruined. It was probably one of the imaginations of the inventive Ctesias, from whom Diodorus evidently derived all the main points of his description.

Thus far there is no great difficulty in identifying the existing remains with buildings mentioned by ancient authors; but, at the point to which we are now come, the subject grows exceedingly obscure, and it is impossible to offer more than reasonable conjectures upon the true character of the remaining ruins. The descriptions of ancient writers would lead us to expect that we should find among the ruins unmistakable traces of the great temple of Belus, and at least some indication of the position occupied by the Hanging Gardens. These two famous constructions can scarcely, one would think, have wholly perished. More especially, the Belus temple, which was a stade square, and (according to some) a stade in height, must almost of necessity have a representative among the existing remains. This, indeed, is admitted on all hands; and the controversy is thereby narrowed to the question, which of two great ruins-the only two entitled by their size and situation to attention-has the better right to be regarded as the great and celebrated sanctuary of the ancient Babylon.

That the mound of Babil is the *ziggurat* or tower of a Babylonian temple scarcely admits of a doubt. Its square shape, its solid construction, its isolated grandeur, its careful emplacement with the sides facing the cardinal points, and its close resemblance to other known Babylonian temple-towers, sufficiently mark it for a building of this character, or at any rate raise a presumption which it would require very strong reasons indeed to overcome. Its size moreover corresponds well with the accounts which have come down to us of the dimensions of the Belus temple, and its name and proximity to the other main ruins show that it belonged certainly to the ancient capital. Against its claim to be regarded as the remains of the temple of Bolus two objections only can be argued: these are the absence of any appearance of stages, or even of a pyramidical shape, from the present ruin, and its position on the same side of the Euphrates with the palace. Herodotus expressly declares that the temple of Belus and the royal palace were upon opposite sides of the river, and states, moreover, that the temple was built in stages, which rose one above the other to the number of eight. Now these two circumstances, which do not belong at present to the Babil mound, attach to a ruin distant from it about eleven or twelve miles —a ruin which is certainly one of the most remarkable in the whole country, and which, if Babylon had really been of the size asserted by Herodotus, might possibly have been included within the walls. The Birs-i-Nimrud had certainly seven, probably eight stages, and it is the only ruin on the present western bank of the Euphrates which is at once sufficiently grand to answer to the descriptions of the Belus temple, and sufficiently near to the other ruin to make its original inclusion within the walls not absolutely impossible. Hence, ever since the attention of scholars was first directed to the subject of Babylonian topography, opinion has been divided on the question before us, and there have not been wanting persons to maintain that the Birs-i-Nimrud is the true temple of Belus, if not also the actual tower of Babel, whose erection led to the confusion of tongues and general dispersion of the sons of Adam.

With this latter identification we are not in the present place concerned. With respect to the view that the Birs is the sanctuary of Belus, it may be observed in the first place that the size of the building is very much smaller than that ascribed to the Belus temple; secondly, that it was dedicated to Kebo, who cannot be identified with Bel; and thirdly, that it is not really any part of the remains of the ancient capital, but belongs to an entirely distinct town. The cylinders found in the ruin by Sir Henry Eawlinson declare the building to have been "the wonder of Borsippa;" and Borsippa, according to all the ancient authorities, was a town by itself-an entirely distinct place from Babylon. To include Borsippa within the outer wall of Babylon is to run counter to all the authorities on the subject, the inscriptions, the native writer, Berosus, and the classical geographers generally. Nor is the position thus assigned to the Belus temple in harmony with the statement of Herodotus, which alone causes explorers to seek for the temple on the west side of the river. For, though the expression which this writer uses does not necessarily mean that the temple was in the exact centre of one of the two divisions of the town, it certainly implies that it lay towards the middle of one division-well within it-and not upon its outskirts. It is indeed inconceivable that the main sanctuary of the place, where the kings constantly offered their worship, should have been nine or ten miles from the palace! The distance between the Amran mound and Babil, which is about two miles, is quite as great as probability will allow us to believe existed between the old residence of the kings and the sacred shrine to which they were in the constant habit of resorting.

Still there remain as objections to the identification of the great temple with the Babil mound the two arguments already noticed. The Babil mound has no appearance of stages such as the Birs presents, nor has it even a pyramidical shape. It is a huge platform with a nearly level top, and sinks, rather than rises, in the centre. What has become, it is asked, of the seven upper stages of the great Belus tower, if this ruin represents it? Whither have they vanished? How is it that in crumbling down they have not left something like a heap towards the middle? To this it may be replied that the destruction of the Belus tower has not been the mere work of the elements-it was violently broken down either by Xerxes, or by some later king, who may have completely removed all the upper stages. Again, it has served as a quarry to the hunters after bricks for more than twenty centuries; so that it is only surprising that it still retains so much of its original shape. Further, when Alexander entered Babylon more than 2000 years ago 10,000 men were employed for several weeks in clearing away the rubbish and laying bare the foundations of the building. It is quite possible that a conical mass of crumbled brick may have been removed from the top of the mound at this time.

The difficulty remains that the Babil mound is on the same side of the Euphrates with the ruins of the Great Palace, whereas Herodotus makes the two buildings balance each other, one on the right and the other on the left bank of the stream. Now here it is in the first place to be observed that Herodotus is the only writer who does this. No other ancient author tells us anything of the relative situation of the two buildings. We have thus nothing to explain but the bald statement of a single writer —a writer no doubt of great authority, but still one not wholly infallible. We might say, then, that Herodotus probably made a mistake-that his memory failed him in this instance, or that he mistook his notes on the subject. Or we may explain his error by supposing that he confounded a canal from the Euphrates, which seems to have anciently passed between the Babil mound and the Kasr (called Shebil by Nebuchadnezzar) with the main stream. Or, finally, we may conceive that at the time of his visit the old palace lay in ruins, and that the palace of Nerig-lissar on the west bank of the stream was that of which he spoke. It is at any rate remarkable, considering how his authority is quoted as fixing the site of the Belus tower to the west bank, that, in the only place where he gives us any intimation of the side of the river on which he would have placed the tower, it is the east and not the west bank to which his words point. He makes those who saw the treachery of Zopyrus at the Belian and Kissian gates, which must have been to the east of the city, at once take refuge in the famous sanctuary, which he implies was in the vicinity.

On the whole, therefore, it seems best to regard the Babil mound as the ziggurat of the great temple of Bel (called by some "the tomb of Belus") which the Persians destroyed and which Alexander intended to restore. With regard to the "hanging gardens," as they were an erection of less than half the size of the tower, it is not so necessary to suppose that distinct traces must remain of them. Their debris may be confused with those of the Kasr mound, on which one writer places them. Or they may have stood between the Kasr and Amran ruins, where are now some mounds of no great height. Or, possibly, their true site is in the modern El Homeira, the remarkable red mound which lies east of the Kasr at the distance of about 800 yards, and attains an elevation of sixty-five feet. Though this building is not situated upon the banks of the Euphrates, where Strabo and Diodorus place the gardens, it abuts upon a long low valley into which the Euphrates water seems formerly to have been introduced, and which may therefore have been given the name of the river. This identification is, however, it must be allowed, very doubtful.

The two lines of mounds which enclose the long low valley above mentioned are probably the remains of an embankment which here confined the waters of a great reservoir. Nebuchadnezzar relates that he constructed a large reservoir, which he calls the Yapur-Shapu, in Babylon, and led water into it by means of an "eastern canal" —the Shebil. The Shebil canal, it is probable, left the Euphrates at some point between Babil and the Kasr, and ran across with a course nearly from west to east to the top of the Yapur-Shapu. This reservoir seems to have been a long and somewhat narrow parallelogram, running nearly from north to south, which shut in the great palace on the east and protected it like a huge moat. Most likely it communicated with the Euphrates towards the south by a second canal, the exact line of which cannot be determined. Thus the palatial residence of the Babylonian kings looked in both directions upon broad sheets of water, an agreeable prospect in so hot a climate; while, at the same time, by the assignment of a double channel to the Euphrates, its floods were the more readily controlled, and the city was preserved from those terrible inundations which in modern times have often threatened the existence of Baghdad.

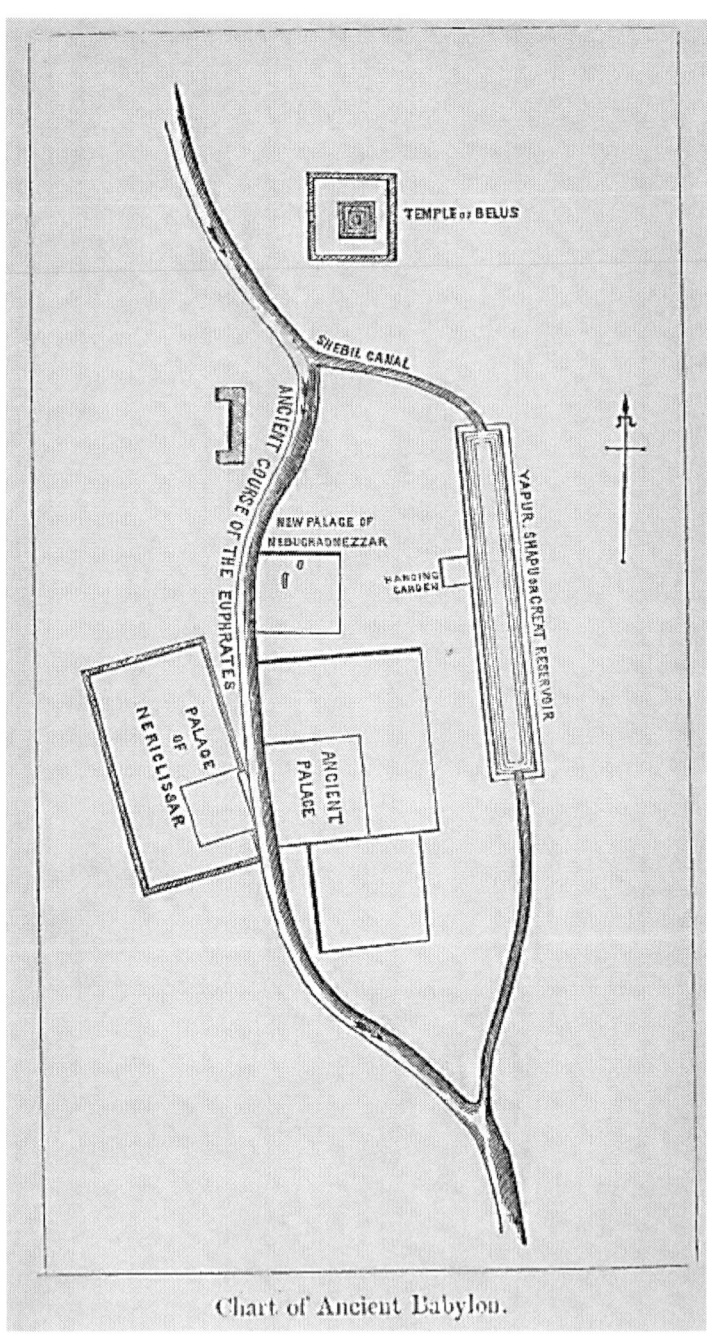

Chart of Ancient Babylon.

The other lines of mound upon the east side of the river may either be Parthian works, or (possibly) they may be the remains of some of those lofty walls whereby, according to Diodorus, the greater palace was surrounded and defended. The fragments of them which remain are so placed that if the lines were produced they would include all the principal ruins on the left bank except the Babil tower. They may therefore be the old defences of the Eastern palace; though, if so, it is strange that they run in lines which are neither straight nor parallel to those of the buildings enclosed by them. The irregularity of these ramparts is certainly a very strong argument in favor of their having been the work of a people considerably more barbarous and ignorant than the Babylonians.

Chapter V. Arts and Sciences

> Τοῦτο γε διαβεβαιώσαιτ' αν τις προσηκόντως, ὅτι Χαλδαιοι μεγίστην εξιν εν αστρολογία απάντων ανθρώπων εχουσι, και διότι πλείστην επιμελειαν εποιησαντο ταύτης της θεωρίας. —Diod. Sic. ii. 31.

That the Babylonians were among the most ingenious of all the nations of antiquity, and had made considerable progress in the arts and sciences before their conquest by the Persians, is generally admitted. The classical writers commonly parallel them with the Egyptians; and though, from their habit of confusing Babylon with Assyria, it is not always quite certain that the inhabitants of the more southern country-the real Babylonians-are meant, still there is sufficient reason to believe that, in the estimation of the Greeks and Romans, the people of the lower Euphrates were regarded as at least equally advanced in civilization with those of the Nile valley and the Delta. The branches of knowledge wherein by general consent the Babylonians principally excelled were architecture and astronomy. Of their architectural works two at least were reckoned among the "Seven Wonders," while others, not elevated to this exalted rank, were yet considered to be among the most curious and admirable of Oriental constructions. In astronomical science they were thought to have far excelled all other nations, and the first Greeks who made much progress in the subject confessed themselves the humble disciples of Babylonian teachers.

In the account, which it is proposed to give, in this place, of Babylonian art and science, so far as they are respectively known to us, the priority will be assigned to art, which is an earlier product of the human mind than science; and among the arts the first place will be given to architecture, as at once the most fundamental of all the fine arts, and the one in which the Babylonians attained their greatest excellence. It is as builders that the primitive Chaldaean people, the progenitors of the Babylonians, first appear before us in history; and it was on his buildings that the great king of the later Empire, Nebuchadnezzar, specially prided himself. When Herodotus visited Babylon he was struck chiefly by its extraordinary edifices; and it is the account which the Greek writers gave of these erections that has, more than anything else, procured for the Babylonians the fame that they possess and the position that they hold among the six or seven leading nations of the old world.

The architecture of the Babylonians seems to have culminated in the Temple. While their palaces, their bridges, their walls, even their private houses were remarkable, their grandest works, their most elaborate efforts, were dedicated to the honor and service, not of man, but of God. The Temple takes in Babylonia the same sort of rank which it has in Egypt and in Greece. It is not, as in Assyria, a mere adjunct of the palace. It stands by itself, in proud independence, as the great building of a city, or a part of a city; it is, if not absolutely larger, at any rate loftier and more conspicuous than any other edifice: it often boasts a magnificent adornment: the value of the offerings which are deposited in it is enormous: in every respect it rivals the palace, while in some it has a decided preeminence. It draws all eyes by its superior height and sometimes by its costly ornamentation; it inspires awe by the religious associations which belong to it; finally, it is a stronghold as well as a place of worship, and may furnish a refuge to thousands in the time of danger.

A Babylonian temple seems to have stood commonly within a walled enclosure. In the case of the great temple of Belus at Babylon, the enclosure is said to have been a square of two stades each way, or, in other words, to have contained an area of thirty acres. The temple itself ordinarily consisted of two parts. Its most essential feature was a *ziggurat*, or tower, which was either square, or at any rate rectangular, and built in stages, the smallest number of such stages being two, and the largest known number seven. At the summit of the tower was probably in every case a shrine, or chapel, of greater or less size, containing altars and images. The ascent to this was on the outside of the towers, which were entirely solid; and it generally wound round the different faces of the towers, ascending them either by means of steps or by an inclined plane. Special care was taken with regard to the emplacement of the tower, either its sides or its angles being made exactly to confront the cardinal points. It is said that the temple-towers were used not merely for religious purposes but also as observatories, a use with a view to which this arrangement of their position would have been serviceable.

Besides the shrine at the summit of the temple-tower or ziggurat, there was commonly at the base of the tower, or at any rate somewhere within the enclosure, a second shrine or chapel, in which the ordinary worshipper, who wished to spare himself the long ascent, made his offerings. Here again the ornamentation was most costly, lavish use being made of the precious metals for images and other furniture. Altars of different sizes were placed in the open air in the vicinity of this lower shrine, on which were sacrificed different classes of victims, gold being used occasionally as the material of the altar.

The general appearance of a Babylonian temple, or at any rate of its chief feature, the tower or *ziggurat*, will be best gathered from a more particular description of a single building of the kind; and the building which it will be most convenient to take for that purpose is that remarkable edifice which strikes moderns with more admiration than any other now existing in the country, and which has also been more completely and more carefully examined than any other Babylonian ruins-the Birs-i-Nimrud, or ancient temple of Nebo at Borsippa. The plan of this tower has been almost completely made out from data still existing on the spot; and a restoration of the original building may be given with a near approach to certainty.

Upon a platform of crude brick, raised a few feet above the level of the alluvial plain, was built the first or basement stage of the great edifice, an exact square, 272 feet each way, and and probably twenty-six feet in perpendicular height. On this was erected a second stage of exactly the same height, but a square of only 230 feet; which however was not placed exactly in the middle of the first, but further from its northeastern than its south-western edge, twelve feet only from the one and thirty feet from the other. The third stage, which was imposed in the same way upon the second, was also twenty-six feet high, and was a square of 188 feet. Thus far the plan had been uniform and without any variety; but at this point an alteration took place. The height of the fourth stage, instead of being twenty-six, was only fifteen feet. In other respects however the old numbers were maintained; the fourth stage was diminished equally with the others, and was consequently a square of 146 feet. It was emplaced upon the stage below it exactly as the former stages had been. The remaining stages probably followed the same rule of diminution-the fifth being a square of 104, the sixth one of 24, and the seventh one of 20 feet. Each of these stages had a height of fifteen feet. Upon the seventh or final stage was erected the shrine or tabernacle, which was probably also fifteen feet high, and about the same length and breadth. Thus the entire height of the building, allowing three feet for the crude brick platform, was 150 feet.

Birs-i-Nimrud, near Babylon.

The ornamentation of the edifice was chiefly by means of color. The seven stages represented the Seven Spheres, in which moved (according to ancient Chaldaean astronomy) the seven planets. To each planet fancy, partly grounding itself upon fact, had from of old assigned a peculiar tint or hue. The Sun was golden, the Moon silver; the distant Saturn, almost beyond the region of light, was black; Jupiter was orange the fiery Mars was red; Venus was a pale Naples yellow; Mercury a deep blue. The seven stages of the tower, like the seven walls of Ecbatana, gave a visible embodiment to these fancies. The basement stage, assigned to Saturn, was blackened by means of a coating of bitumen spread over the face of the masonry; the second stage, assigned to Jupiter, obtained the appropriate orange color by means of a facing of burnt bricks of that hue; the third stage, that of Mars, was made blood-red by the use of half-burnt bricks formed of a bright red clay; the fourth stage, assigned to the Sun, appears to have been actually covered with thin plates of gold; the fifth, the stage of Venus, received a pale yellow tint from the employment of bricks of that hue; the sixth, the sphere of Mercury, was given an azure tint by vitrifaction, the whole stage having been subjected to an intense heat after it was erected, whereby the bricks composing it were converted into a mass of blue slag; the seventh stage, that of the Moon, was probably, like the fourth, coated with actual plates of metal. Thus the building rose up in stripes of varied color, arranged almost as nature's cunning arranges hues in the rainbow, tones of red coming first, succeeded by a broad stripe of yellow, the yellow being followed by blue. Above this the glowing silvery summit melted into the bright sheen of the sky.

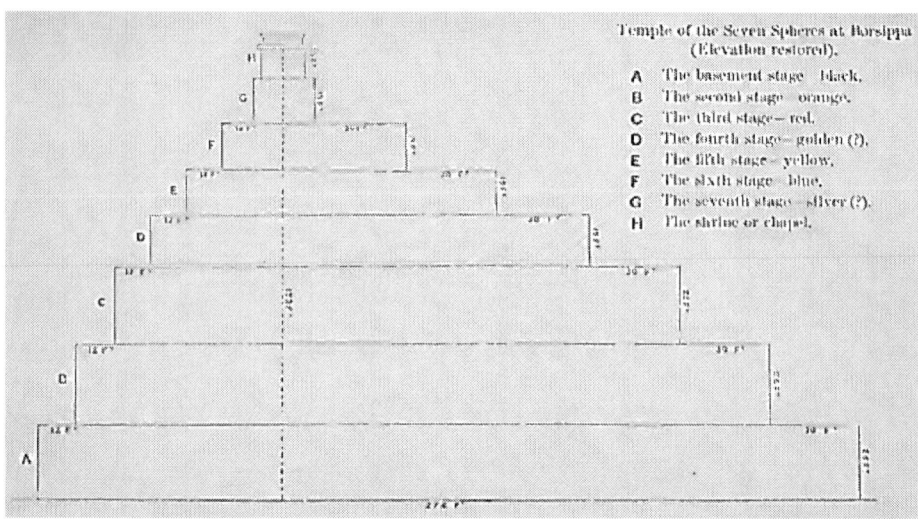

The faces of the various stages were, as a general rule, flat and unbroken, unless it were by a stair or ascent, of which however there has been found no trace. But there were two exceptions to this general plainness. The basement stage was indented with a number of shallow squared recesses, which seem to have been intended for a decoration. The face of the third stage was weak on account of its material, which was brick but half-burnt. Here then the builders, not for ornament's sake, but to strengthen their work, gave to the wall the support of a number of shallow buttresses. They also departed from their usual practice, by substituting for the rigid perpendicular of the other faces a slight slope outwards for some distance from the base. These arrangements, which are apparently part of the original work, and not remedies applied subsequently, imply considerable knowledge of architectural principles on the part of the builders, and no little ingenuity in turning architectural resources to account.

With respect to the shrine which was emplaced upon the topmost, or silver stage, little is definitely known. It appears to have been of brick; and we may perhaps conclude from the analogy of the old Chaldaean shrines at the summits of towers, as well as from that of the Belus shrine at Babylon, that it was richly ornamented both within and without; but it is impossible to state anything as to the exact character of the ornamentation.

The tower is to be regarded as fronting to the north-east, the coolest side and that least exposed to the sun's rays from the time that they become oppressive in Babylonia. On this side was the ascent, which consisted probably of abroad staircase extending along the whole front of the building. The side platforms (those towards the south-east and north-west) —at any rate of the first and second stages, probably of all-were occupied by a series of chambers abutting upon the perpendicular wall, as the priests' chambers of Solomon's temple abutted upon the side walls of that building. In these were doubtless lodged the priests and other attendants upon the temple service. The side chambers seem sometimes to have communicated with vaulted apartments within the solid mass of the structure, like those of which we hear in the structure supporting the "hanging gardens." It is possible that there may have been internal stair-cases, connecting the vaulted apartments of one stage with those of another; but the ruin has not yet been sufficiently explored for us to determine whether or not there was such communication.

The great Tower is thought to have been approached through a vestibule of considerable size. Towards the north-east the existing ruin is prolonged in an irregular manner and it is imagined that this prolongation marks the site of a vestibule or propylaeum, originally distinct from the tower, but now, through the crumbling down of both buildings, confused with its ruins. As no scientific examination has been made of this part of the mound, the above supposition can only be regarded as a conjecture. Possibly the excrescence does not so much mark a vestibule as a second shrine, like that which is said to have existed at the foot of the Belus Tower at Babylon. Till, however, additional researches have been made, it is in vain to think of restoring the plan or elevation of this part of the temple.

From the temples of the Babylonians we may now pass to their palaces-constructions inferior in height and grandeur, but covering a greater space, involving a larger amount of labor, and admitting of more architectural variety. Unfortunately the palaces have suffered from the ravages of time even more than the temples, and in considering their plan and character we obtain little help from the existing remains. Still, something may be learnt of them from this source, and where it fails we may perhaps be allowed to eke out the scantiness of our materials by drawing from the elaborate descriptions of Diodorus such points as have probability in their favor.

The Babylonian palace, like the Assyrian, and the Susianian, stood upon a lofty mound or platform. This arrangement provided at once for safety, for enjoyment, and for health. It secured a pure air, freedom from the molestation of insects, and a position only assailable at a few points. The ordinary shape of the palace mound appears to have been square; its elevation was probably not less than fifty or sixty feet. It was composed mainly of sun-dried bricks, which however were almost certainly enclosed externally by a facing of burnt brick, and may have been further strengthened within by walls of the same material, which perhaps traversed the whole mound. The entire mass seems to have been carefully drained, and the collected waters were conveyed through subterranean channels to the level of the plain at the mound's base. The summit of the platform was no doubt paved, either with stone or burnt brick-mainly, it is probable, with the latter; since the former material was scarce, and though a certain number of stone pavement slabs have been found, they are too rare and scattered to imply anything like the general use of stone paving. Upon the platform, most likely towards the centre, rose the actual palace, not built (like the Assyrian palaces) of crude brick faced with a better material, but constructed wholly of the finest and hardest burnt brick laid in a mortar of extreme tenacity, with walls of enormous thickness, parallel to the sides of the mound, and meeting each other at right angles. Neither the ground-plan nor the elevation of a Babylonian palace can be given; nor can even a conjectural restoration of such a building be made, since the small fragment of Nebuchadnezzar's palace which remains has defied all attempts to reduce it to system. We can only say that the lines of the building were straight; that the walls rose, at any rate to a considerable height, without windows; and that the flatness of the straight line was broken by numerous buttressses and pilasters. We have also evidence that occasionally there was an ornamentation of the building, either within or without, by means of sculptured stone slabs, on which were represented figures of a small size, carefully wrought. The general ornamentation, however, external as well as internal, we may well believe to have been such as Diodorus states, colored representations on brick of war-scenes, and hunting-scenes, the counterparts in a certain sense of those magnificent bas-reliefs which everywhere clothed the walls of palaces in Assyria. It has been already noticed that abundant remains of such representations have been found upon the Kasr mound. They seem to have alternated with cuneiform inscriptions, in white on a blue ground, or else with a patterning of rosettes in the same colors.

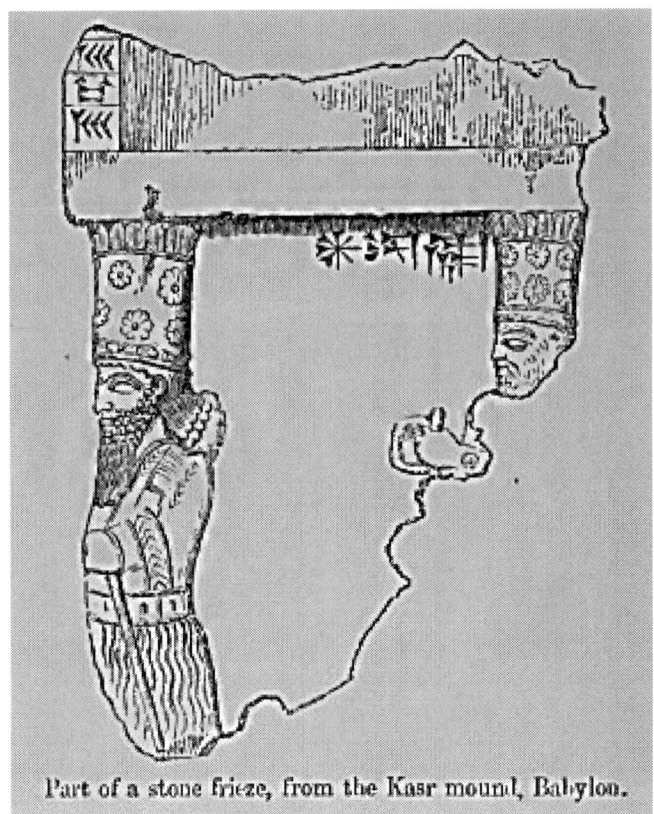

Part of a stone frieze, from the Kasr mound, Babylon.

Of the general arrangement of the royal palaces, of their height, their number of stories, their roofing, and their lighting, we know absolutely nothing. The statement made by Herodotus, that many of the private houses in the town had three or four stories, would naturally lead us to suppose that the palaces were built similarly; but no ancient author tells us that this was so. The fact that the walls which exist, though of considerable height, show no traces of windows, would seem to imply that the lighting, as in Assyria, was from the top of the apartment, either from the ceiling, or from apertures in the part of the walls adjoining the ceiling. Altogether, such evidence as exists favors the notion that the Babylonian palace, in its character and general arrangements, resembled the Assyrian, with only the two differences, that Babylonian was wholly constructed of burnt brick, while in the Assyrian the sun-dried material was employed to a large extent; and, further, that in Babylonia the decoration of the walls was made, not by slabs of alabaster, which did not exist in the country, but mainly-almost entirely-by colored representations upon the brickwork.

Among the adjuncts of the principal palace at Babylon was the remarkable construction known to the Greeks and Romans as "the Hanging Garden." The accounts which, Diodorus, Strabo, and Q. Curtius give of this structure are not perhaps altogether trustworthy; still, it is probable that they are in the main at least founded on fact. We may safely believe that a lofty structure was raised at Babylon on several tiers of arches, which supported at the top a mass of earth, wherein grew, not merely flowers and shrubs, but trees of a considerable size. The Assyrians had been in the habit of erecting structures of a somewhat similar kind, artificial elevations to support a growth of trees and shrubs; but they were content to place their garden at the summit of a single row of pillars or arches, and thus to give it a very moderate height. At Babylon the object was to produce an artificial imitation of a mountain. For this purpose several tiers of arches were necessary; and these appear to have been constructed in the manner of a Roman amphitheatre, one directly over another so that the outer wall formed from summit to base a single perpendicular line. Of the height of the structure various accounts are given, while no writer reports the number of the tiers of arches. Hence there are no sufficient data for a reconstruction of the edifice.

Of the walls and bridge of Babylon, and of the ordinary houses of the people, little more is known than has been already reported in the general description of the capital. It does not appear that they possessed any very great architectural merit. Some skill was shown in constructing the piers of the bridge, which presented an angle to the current and then a curved line, along which the water slid gently. The loftiness of the houses, which were of three or four stories, is certainly surprising, since Oriental houses have very rarely more than two stories. Their construction, however, seems to have been rude; and the pillars especially-posts of palm, surrounded with wisps of rushes, and then plastered and painted-indicate a low condition of taste and a poor and coarse style of domestic architecture.

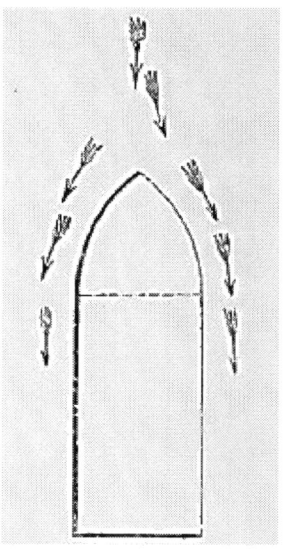

The material used by the Babylonians in their constructions seems to have been almost entirely brick. Like the early Chaldaeans, they employed bricks of two kinds, both the ruder sun-dried sort, and the very superior kiln-baked article. The former, however, was only applied to platforms, and to the interior of palace mounds and of very thick walls, and was never made by the later people the sole material of a building. In every case there was at least a revetement of kiln-dried brick, while the grander buildings were wholly constructed of it. The baked bricks used were of several different qualities, and (within rather narrow limits) of different sizes. The finest quality of brick was yellow, approaching to our Stourbridge or fire-brick; another very hard kind was blue, approaching to black; the commoner and coarser sorts were pink or red, and these were sometimes, though rarely, but half-baked, in which case they were weak and friable. The shape was always square; and the dimensions varied between twelve and fourteen inches for the length and breadth, and between three and four inches for the thickness. At the corners of buildings, half-bricks were used in the alternate rows, since otherwise the joinings must have been all one exactly over another. The bricks were always made with a mold, and were commonly stamped on one face with an inscription. They were, of course, ordinarily laid horizontally. Sometimes, however, there was a departure from this practice. Rows of bricks were placed vertically, separated from one another by single horizontal layers. This arrangement seems to have been regarded as conducing to strength, since it occurs only where there is an evident intention of supporting a weak construction by the use of special architectural expedients.

Babylonian brick.

The Babylonian builders made use of three different kinds of cement. The most indifferent was crude clay, or mud, which was mixed with chopped straw, to give it greater tenacity, and was applied in layers of extraordinary thickness. This was (it is probable) employed only where it was requisite that the face of the building should have a certain color. A cement superior to clay, but not of any very high value, unless as a preventive against damp, was bitumen, which was very generally used in basements and in other structures exposed to the action of water. Mortar, however, or lime cement was far more commonly employed than either of the others, and was of very excellent quality, equal indeed to the best Roman material.

There can be no doubt that the general effect of the more ambitious efforts of the Babylonian architects was grand and imposing. Even now, in their desolation and ruin, their great size renders them impressive; and there are times and states of atmosphere under which they fill the beholder with a sort of admiring awe, akin to the feeling which is called forth by the contemplation of the great works of nature. Rude and inartificial in their idea and general construction, without architectural embellishment, without variety, without any beauty of form, they yet affect men by their mere mass, producing a direct impression of sublimity, and at the same time arousing a sentiment of wonder at the indomitable perseverance which from materials so unpromising could produce such gigantic results. In their original condition, when they were adorned with color, with a lavish display of the precious metals, with pictured representations of human life, and perhaps with statuary of a rough kind, they must have added to the impression produced by size a sense of richness and barbaric magnificence. The African spirit, which loves gaudy hues and costly ornament, was still strong among the Babylonians, even after they had been Semitized; and by the side of Assyria, her colder and more correct northern sister, Babylonia showed herself a true child of the south-rich, glowing, careless of the laws of taste, bent on provoking admiration by the dazzling brilliancy of her appearance.

It is difficult to form a decided opinion as to the character of Babylonian mimetic art. The specimens discovered are so few, so fragmentary, and in some instances so worn by time and exposure, that we have scarcely the means of doing justice to the people in respect of this portion of their civilization. Setting aside the intaglios on seals and gems, which have such a general character of quaintness and grotesqueness, or at any rate of formality, that we can scarcely look upon many of them as the serious efforts of artists doing their best, we possess not half a dozen specimens of the mimetic art of the people in question. We have one sculpture in the round, one or two modelled clay figures, a few bas-reliefs, one figure of a king engraved on stone, and a few animal forms represented the same material. Nothing more has reached us but fragments of pictorial representations too small for criticism to pronounce upon, and descriptions of ancient writers too incomplete to be of any great value.

The single Babylonian sculpture in the round which has come down to our times is the colossal lion standing over the prostrate figure of a man, which is still to be seen on the Kasr mound, as has been already mentioned. The accounts of travellers uniformly state that it is a work of no merit-either barbarously executed, or left unfinished by the sculptor-and probably much worn by exposure to the weather. A sketch made by a recent visitor and kindly communicated to the author, seems to show that, while the general form of the animal was tolerably well hit off, the proportions were in some respects misconceived, and the details not only rudely but incorrectly rendered. The extreme shortness of the legs and the extreme thickness of the tail are the most prominent errors; there is also great awkwardness in the whole representation of the beast's shoulder. The head is so mutilated that it is impossible to do more than conjecture its contour. Still the whole figure is not without a certain air of grandeur and majesty.

Lion, standing over a prostrate man (Babylon).

The human appears to be inferior to the animal form. The prostrate man is altogether shapeless, and can never, it would seem, have been very much better than it is at the present time.

Modelled figures in clay are of rare occurrence. The best is one figured by Ker Porter, which represents a mother with a child in her arms. The mother is seated in a natural and not ungraceful attitude on a rough square pedestal. She is naked except for a hood, or mantilla, which covers the head, shoulders, and back, and a narrow apron which hangs down in front. She wears earrings and a bracelet. The child, which sleeps on her left shoulder, wears a shirt open in front, and a short but full tunic, which is gathered into plaits. Both figures are in simple and natural taste, but the limbs of the infant are somewhat too thin and delicate. The statuette is about three inches and a half high, and shows signs of having been covered with a tinted glaze.

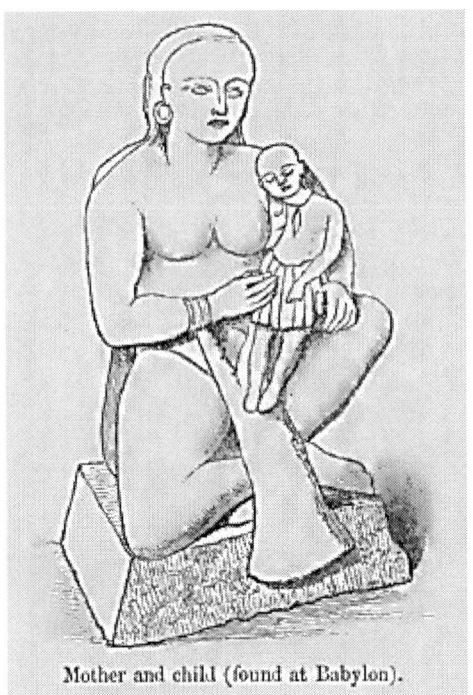
Mother and child (found at Babylon).

The single figure of a king which we possess is clumsy and ungraceful.

Figure of a Babylonian king, probably Merodach-iddin-akhi.

It is chiefly remarkable for the elaborate ornamentation of the head-dress and the robes, which have a finish equal to that of the best Assyrian specimens. The general proportions are not bad; but the form is stiff, and the drawing of the right hand is peculiarly faulty, since it would be scarcely possible to hold arrows in the manner represented.

Figure of a dog (from a black stone of the time of Merodach-iddin-akhi, found at Babylon).

Figure of a bird (from the same stone).

The engraved animal forms have a certain amount of merit. The figure of a dog sitting, which is common on the "black stones," is drawn with spirit; and a bird, sometimes regarded as a cock, but more resembling a bustard, is touched with a delicate hand, and may be pronounced superior to any Assyrian representation of the feathered tribe. The hound on a bas-relief, given in the first volume of this work, is also good; and the cylinders exhibit figures of goats, cows, deer, and even monkeys, which are truthful and meritorious.

Animal forms (from the cylinders).

It has been observed that the main characteristic of the engravings on gems and cylinders, considered as works of mimetic art, is their quaintness and grotesqueness. A few specimens, taken almost at random from the admirable collection of M. Felix Lajard, will sufficiently illustrate this feature.

Grotesque figures of men and animals (from a cylinder).

In one the central position is occupied by a human figure whose left arm has two elbow-joints, while towards the right two sitting figures threaten one another with their fists, in the upper quarter, and in the lower two nondescript animals do the same with their jaws. The entire drawing of this design seems to be intentionally rude. The faces of the main figures are evidently intended to be ridiculous; and the heads of the two animals are extravagantly grotesque. On another cylinder three nondescript animals play the principal part. One of them is on the point of taking into his mouth the head of a man who vainly tries to escape by flight. Another, with the head of a pike, tries to devour the third, which has the head of a bird and the body of a goat.

Men and monsters (from a cylinder).

This kind intention seems to be disputed by a naked man with a long beard, who seizes the fish-headed monster with his right hand, and at the same time administers from behind a severe kick with his right foot. The heads of the three main monsters, the tail and trousers of the principal one, and the whole of the small figure in front of the flying man, are exceedingly quaint, and remind one of the pencil of Fuseli.

Serio-comic drawing (from a cylinder).

The third of the designs approaches nearly to the modern caricature. It is a drawing in two portions. The upper line of figures represents a procession of worshippers who bear in solemn state their offerings to a god. In the lower line this occupation is turned to a jest. Nondescript animals bring with a serio-comic air offerings which consist chiefly of game, while a man in a mask seeks to steal away the sacred tree from the temple wherein the scene is enacted.

It is probable that the most elaborate and most artistic of the Babylonian works of art were of a kind which has almost wholly perished. What bas-relief was to the Assyrian, what painting is to moderns, that enamelling upon brick appears to have been to the people of Babylon. The mimetic power, which delights in representing to itself the forms and actions of men, found a vent in this curious byway of the graphic art; and the images of the Chaldaeans, portrayed upon the wall, with vermilion, and other hues, formed the favorite adornment of palaces and public buildings, at once employing the artist, gratifying the taste of the native connoisseur, and attracting the admiration of the foreigner.

The artistic merit of these works can only be conjectured. The admiration of the Jews, or even that of Diodorus, who must be viewed here as the echo of Ctesias, is no sure test; for the Jews were a people very devoid of true artistic appreciation; and Ctesias was bent on exaggerating the wonders of foreign countries to the Greeks. The fact of the excellence of Assyrian art at a somewhat earlier date lends however support to the view that the wall-painting of the Babylonians had some real artistic excellence. We can scarcely suppose that there was any very material difference, in respect of taste and aesthetic power, between the two cognate nations, or that the Babylonians under Nebuchadnezzar fell very greatly short of the Assyrians under

Asshur-bani-pal. It is evident that the same subjects-war scenes and hunting scenes-approved themselves to both people; and it is likely that their treatment was not very different. Even in the matter of color, the contrast was not sharp nor strong; for the Assyrians partially colored their bas-reliefs.

Tho tints chiefly employed by the Babylonians in their colored representations were white, blue, yellow, brown, and black. The blue was of different shades, sometimes bright and deep, sometimes exceedingly pale. The yellow was somewhat dull, resembling our yellow ochre. The brown was this same hue darkened. In comparatively rare instances the Babylonians made use of a red, which they probably obtained with some difficulty. Objects were colored, as nearly as possible, according to their natural tints-water a light blue, ground yellow, the shafts of spears black, lions a tawny brown, etc. No attempt was made to shade the figures or the landscape, much less to produce any general effect by means of *chiaroscuro*; but the artist trusted for his effect to a careful delineation of forms, and a judicious arrangement of simple hues.

Considerable metallurgic knowledge and skill were shown in the composition of the pigments, and the preparation and application of the glaze wherewith they are covered. The red used was a sub-oxide of copper; the yellow was sometimes oxide of iron, sometimes antimoniate of lead-the Naples yellow of modern artists; the blue was either cobalt or oxide of copper; the white was oxide of tin. Oxide of load was added in some cases, not as a coloring matter, but as a flux, to facilitate the fusion of the glaze. In other cases the pigment used was covered with a vitreous coat of an alkaline silicate of alumina.

The pigments were not applied to an entirely flat surface. Prior to the reception of the coloring matter and the glaze, each brick was modelled by the hand, the figures being carefully traced out, and a slight elevation given to the more important objects. A very low bas-relief was thus produced, to which the colors were subsequently applied, and the brick was then baked in the furnace.

It is conjectured that the bricks were not modelled singly and separately. A large mass of clay was (it is thought) taken, sufficient to contain a whole subject, or at any rate a considerable portion of a subject. On this the modeller made out his design in low relief. The mass of clay was then cut up into bricks, and each brick was taken and painted separately with the proper colors, after which they were all placed in the furnace and baked. When baked, they were restored to their original places in the design, a thin layer of the finest mortar serving to keep them in place.

From the mimetic art of the Babylonians, and the branches of knowledge connected with it, we may now pass to the purely mechanical arts-as the art by which hard stones were cut, and those of agriculture, metallurgy, pottery, weaving, carpet-making, embroidery, and the like.

The stones shaped, bored, and engraved by Babylonian artisans were not merely the softer and more easily worked kinds, as alabaster, serpentine, and lapis-lazuli, but also the harder sorts-cornelian, agate, quartz, jasper, sienite, loadstone, and green felspar or amazon-stone. These can certainly not have been cut without emery, and scarcely without such devices as rapidly revolving points, or discs, of the kind used by modern lapidaries. Though the devices are in general rude, the work is sometimes exceedingly delicate, and implies a complete mastery over tools and materials, as well as a good deal of artistic power. As far as the mechanical part of the art goes, the Babylonians may challenge comparison with the most advanced of the nations of antiquity; they decidedly excel the Egyptians, and fall little, if at all, short of the Greeks and Romans.

The extreme minuteness of the work in some of the Babylonian seals and gems raises a suspicion that they must have been engraved by the help of a powerful magnifying-glass. A lens has been found in Assyria; and there is much reason to believe that the convenience was at least as well known in the lower country. Glass was certainly in use, and was cut into such shapes as were required. It is at any rate exceedingly likely that magnifying-glasses, which were undoubtedly known to the Greeks in the time of Aristophanes, were employed by the artisans of Babylon during the most flourishing period of the Empire.

Of Babylonian metal-work we have scarcely any direct means of judging. The accounts of ancient authors imply that the Babylonians dealt freely with the material, using gold and silver for statues, furniture, and utensils, bronze for gates and images, and iron sometimes for the latter. We may assume that they likewise employed bronze and iron for tools and weapons, since those metals were certainly so used by the Assyrians. Lead was made of service in building; where iron was also employed, if great strength was needed. The golden images are said to have been sometimes solid, in which case we must suppose them to have been cast in a mold; but undoubtedly in most cases the gold was a mere external covering, and was applied in plates, which were hammered into shape upon some cheaper substance below. Silver was no doubt used also in plates, more especially when applied externally to walls, or internally to the woodwork of palaces; but the silver images, ornamental figures, and utensils of which we hear, were most probably solid. The bronze works must have been remarkable. We are told that both the town and the palace gates were of this material, and it is implied that the latter were too heavy to be opened in the ordinary manner. Castings on an enormous scale would be requisite for such purposes; and the Babylonians must thus have possessed the art of running into a single mold vast masses of metal.

Gate and gateway (from a cylinder).

Probably the gates here mentioned were solid; but occasionally, it would seem, the Babylonians had gates of a different kind, composed of a number of perpendicular bars, united by horizontal ones above and below. They had also, it would appear, metal gateways of a similar character.

The metal-work of personal ornaments, such as bracelets and armlets, and again that of dagger handles, seems to have resembled the work of the Assyrians.

Small figures in bronze were occasionally cast by the Babylonians, which were sometimes probably used as amulets, while perhaps more generally they wore mere ornaments of houses, furniture, and the like. Among these may be noticed figures of dogs in a sitting posture, much resembling the dog represented among the constellations, figures of men, grotesque in character, and figures of monsters. An interesting specimen, which combines a man and a monster, was found by Sir R. Ker Porter at Babylon.

Bronze ornament (found at Babylon).

The pottery of the Babylonians was of excellent quality, and is scarcely to be distinguished from the Assyrian, which it resembles alike in form and in material. The bricks of the best period were on the whole better than any used in the sister country, and may compare for hardness and fineness with the best Roman. The earthenware is of a fine terra-cotta, generally of a light red color, and slightly baked, but occasionally of a yellow hue, with a tinge of green. It consists of cups, jars, vases, and other vessels.

Vases and jug (from the cylinders).

They appear to have been made upon the wheel, and are in general unornamented. From representations upon the cylinders, it appears that the shapes were often elegant. Long and narrow vases with thin necks seem to have been used for water vessels; these had rounded or pointed bases, and required therefore the support of a stand. Thin jugs were also in use, with slight elegant handles.

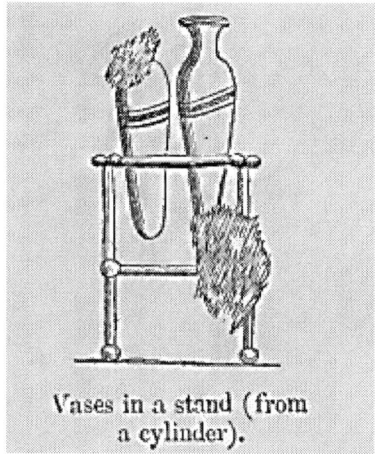

Vases in a stand (from a cylinder).

It is conjectured that sometimes modelled figures may have been introduced at the sides as handles to the vases; but neither the cylinders nor the extant remains confirm this supposition. The only ornamentation hitherto observed consists in a double band which seems to have been carried round some of the vases in an incomplete spiral. The vases sometimes have two handles; but they are plain and small, adding nothing to the beauty of the vessels. Occasionally the whole vessel is glazed with a rich blue color.

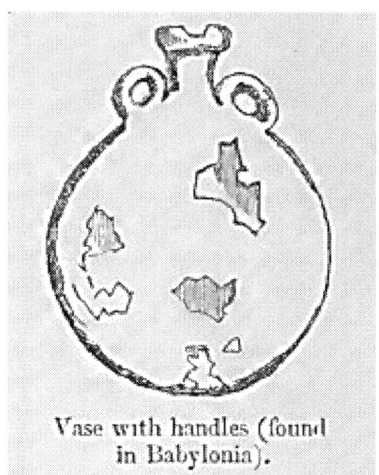

Vase with handles (found in Babylonia).

The Babylonians certainly employed glass for vessels for a small size. They appear not to have been very skilful blowers, since their bottles are not unfrequently misshappen. They generally stained their glass with, some coloring matter, and occasionally ornamented it with a ribbing. Whether they were able to form masses of glass of any considerable size, whether they used it, like the Egyptians, for beads and bugles, or for mosaics, is uncertain.

77

Babylonian glass bottles.

If we suppose a foundation in fact for Pliny's story of the great emerald (?) presented by a king of Babylon to an Egyptian Pharaoh, we must conclude that very considerable masses of glass were produced by the Babylonians, at least occasionally; for the said emerald, which can scarcely have been of any other material, was four cubits (or six feet) long and three cubits (or four and a half feet) broad.

Of all the productions of the Babylonians none obtained such, high repute in ancient times as their textile fabrics. Their carpets especially were of great celebrity, and were largely exported to foreign countries. They were dyed of various colors, and represented objects similar to those found on the gems, as griffins and such like monsters. Their position in the ancient world may be compared to that which is now borne by the fabrics of Turkey and Persia, which are deservedly preferred to those of all other countries.

Next to their carpets, the highest, character was borne by their muslins. Formed of the finest cotton, and dyed of the most brilliant colors, they seemed to the Oriental the very best possible material for dress. The Persian kings preferred them for their own wear; and they had an early fame in foreign countries at a considerable distance from Babylonia. It is probable that they were sometimes embroidered with delicate patterns, such as those which may be seen on the garments of the early Babylonian kings.

Besides woollen and cotton fabrics, the Babylonians also manufactured a good deal of linen cloth, the principal seat of the manufacture being Borsippa. This material was produced, it is probable, chiefly for home consumption, long linen robes being generally worn by the people.

From the arts of the Babylonians we may now pass to their science-an obscure subject, but one which possesses more than common interest. If the classical writers were correct in their belief that Chaldaea was the birthplace of Astronomy, and that their own astronomical science was derived mainly from this quarter, it must be well worth inquiry what the amount of knowledge was which the Babylonians attained on the subject, and what were the means whereby they made their discoveries.

On the broad flat plains of Chaldsea, where the entire celestial hemisphere is continually visible to every eye, and the clear transparent atmosphere shows night after night the heavens gemmed with countless stars, each shining with a brilliancy unknown in our moist northern climes, the attention of man was naturally turned earlier than elsewhere to these luminous bodies, and attempts were made to grasp, and reduce to scientific form, the array of facts which nature presented to the eye in a confused and tangled mass. It required no very long course of observation to acquaint men with a truth, which at first sight none would have suspected-namely, that the luminous points whereof the sky was full were of two kinds, some always maintaining the same position relatively to one another, while others were constantly changing their places, and as it were wandering about the sky. It is certain that the Babylonians at a very early date distinguished from the fixed stars those remarkable five, which, from their wandering propensities, the Greeks called the "planets," and which are the only erratic stars that the naked eye, or that even the telescope, except at a very high power, can discern. With these five they were soon led to class the Moon, which was easily observed to be a wandering luminary, changing her place among the fixed stars with remarkable rapidity. Ultimately, it came to be perceived that the Sun too rose and set at different parts of the year in the neighborhood of different constellations, and that consequently the great luminary was itself also a wanderer, having a path in the sky which it was possible, by means of careful observation, to mark out.

But to do this, to mark out with accuracy the courses of the Sun and Moon among the fixed stars, it was necessary, or at least convenient, to arrange the stars themselves into groups. Thus, too, and thus only, was it possible to give form and order to the chaotic confusion in which the stars seem at first sight to lie, owing to the irregularity of their intervals, the difference in their magnitude, and their apparent countlessness. The most uneducated eye, when raised to the starry heavens on a clear night, fixes here and there upon groups of stars: in the north, Cassiopeia, the Great Bear, the Pleiades-below the Equator, the Southern Cross-must at all times have impressed those who beheld them with a certain sense of unity. Thus the idea of a "constellation" is formed; and this once done, the mind naturally progresses in the same direction, and little by little the whole sky is mapped out into certain portions or districts to which names are given-names taken from some resemblance, real or fancied, between the shapes of the several groups and objects familiar to the early observers. This branch of practical astronomy is termed "uranography" by moderns; its utility is very considerable; thus and thus only can we particularize the individual stars of which we wish to speak; thus and thus only can we retain in our memory the general arrangement of the stars and their positions relatively to each other.

There is reason to believe that in the early Babylonian astronomy the subject of uranography occupied a prominent place. The Chaldaean astronomers not only seized on and named those natural groups which force themselves upon the eye, but artificially arranged the whole heavens into a certain number of constellations or asterisms. The very system of uranography which maintains itself to the present day on our celestial globes and maps, and which is still acknowledged-albeit under protest-in the nomenclature of scientific astronomers, came in all probability from this source, reaching us from the Arabians, who took it from the Greeks who derived it from the Babylonians.

Top of conical stone, bearing figures of constellations.

The Zodiacal constellations at any rate, or those through which the sun's course lies would seem to have had this origin; and many of them may be distinctly recognized on Babylonian monuments which are plainly of a stellar character. The accompanying representation, taken from a conical black stone in the British Museum, and belonging to the twelfth century before our era, is not perhaps, strictly speaking, a zodiac, but it is almost certainly an arrangement of constellations according to the forms assigned them in Babylonian uranography. The Ram, the Bull, the Scorpion, the Serpent, the Dog, the Arrow, the Eagle or Vulture may all be detected on the stone in question, as may similar forms variously arranged on other similar monuments.

Babylonian Zodiac (?)

The Babylonians called the Zodiacal constellations the "Houses of the Sun," and distinguished from them another set of asterisms, which they denominated the "Houses of the Moon." As the Sun and Moon both move through the sky in nearly the same plane, the path of the Moon merely crossing and recrossing that of the Sun, but never diverging from it further than a few degrees, it would seem that these "Houses of the Moon," or lunar asterisms, must have been a division of the Zodiacal stars different from that employed with respect to the sun, either in the number of the "Houses," or in the point of separation between "House" and "House."

The Babylonians observed and calculated eclipses; but their power of calculation does not seem to have been based on scientific knowledge, nor to have necessarily implied sound views as to the nature of eclipses or as to the size, distance, and real motions of the heavenly bodies. The knowledge which they possessed was empirical. Their habits of observation led them to discover the period of 223 lunations or 18 years 10 days, after which eclipses-especially those of the the moon-recur again in the same order. Their acquaintance with this cycle would enable them to predict lunar eclipses with accuracy for many ages, and solar eclipses without much inaccuracy for the next cycle or two.

That the Babylonians carefully noted and recorded eclipses is witnessed by Ptolemy, who had access to a continuous series of such observations reaching back from his own time to B.C. 747. Five of these-all eclipses of the moon-were described by Hipparchus from Babylonian sources, and are found to answer all the requirements of modern science. They belong to the years B.C. 721, 720, 621, and 523. One of them, that of B.C. 721, was total at Babylon. The others were partial, the portion of the moon obscured varying from one digit to seven.

There is no reason to think that the observation of eclipses by the Babylonians commenced with Nabonassar. Ptolemy indeed implies that the series extant in his day went no higher; but this is to be accounted for by the fact, which Berosus mentioned, that Nabonassar destroyed, as far as he was able, the previously existing observations, in order that exact chronology might commence with his own reign.

Other astronomical achievements of the Babylonians were the following. They accomplished a catalogue of the fixed stars, of which the Greeks made use in compiling their stellar tables. They observed and recorded their observations upon occultations of the planets by the sun and moon. They invented the *gnomon* and the *polos*, two kinds of sundial, by means of which they were able to measure time during the day, and to fix the true length of the solar day, with sufficient accuracy. They determined correctly within a small fraction the length of the synodic revolution of the moon. They knew that the true length of the solar year was 365 days and a quarter, nearly. They noticed comets, which they believed to be permanent bodies, revolving in orbits like those of the planets, only greater. They ascribed eclipses of the sun to the interposition of the moon between the sun and the earth. They had notions not far from the truth with respect to the relative distance from the earth of the sun, moon, and planets. Adopting, as was natural, a geocentric system, they decided that the Moon occupied the position nearest to the earth; that beyond the Moon was Mercury, beyond Mercury Venus, beyond Venus Mars, beyond Mars Jupiter, and beyond Jupiter, in the remotest position of all, Saturn. This arrangement was probably based upon a knowledge, more or less exact, of the periodic times which the several bodies occupy in their (real or apparent) revolutions. From the difference in the times the Babylonians assumed a corresponding difference in the size of the orbits, and consequently a greater or less distance from the common centre.

Thus far the astronomical achievements of the Babylonians rest upon the express testimony of ancient writers —a testimony confirmed in many respects by the monuments already deciphered. It is suspected that, when the astronomical tablets which exist by hundreds in the British Museum come to be thoroughly understood, it will be found that the acquaintance of the Chaldaean sages with astronomical phenomena, if not also with astronomical laws, went considerably beyond the point at which we should place it upon the testimony of the Greek and Roman writers. There is said to be distinct evidence that they observed the four satellites of Jupiter, and strong reason to believe that they were acquainted likewise with the seven satellites of Saturn. Moreover, the general laws of the movements of the heavenly bodies seem to have been so far known to them that they could state by anticipation the position of the various planets throughout the year.

In order to attain the astronomical knowledge which they seem to have possessed, the Babylonians must undoubtedly have employed a certain number of instruments. The invention of sun-dials, as already observed, is distinctly assigned to them. Besides these contrivances for measuring time during the day, it is almost certain that they must have possessed means of measuring time during the night. The clepsydra, or water-clock, which was in common use among the Greeks as early as the fifth century before our era, was probably introduced into Greece from the East, and is likely to have been a Babylonian invention. The astrolabe, an instrument for measuring the altitude of stars above the horizon, which was known to Ptolemy, may also reasonably be assigned to them. It has generally been assumed that they were wholly ignorant of the telescope. But if the satellites of Saturn are really mentioned, as it is thought that they are, upon some of the tablets, it will follow-strange as it may seem to us-that the Babylonians possessed optical instruments of the nature of telescopes, since it is impossible, even in the clear and vapor-loss sky of Chaldaea, to discern the faint moons of that distant planet without lenses. A lens, it must be remembered, with a fair magnifying power, has been discovered among the Mesopotamian ruins. A people ingenious enough to discover the magnifying-glass would be naturally led on to the invention of its opposite. When once lenses of the two contrary kinds existed, the elements of a telescope were in being. We could not assume from these data that the discovery was made; but if it shall ultimately be substantiated that bodies invisible to the naked eye were observed by the Babylonians, we need feel no difficulty in ascribing to them the possession of some telescopic instrument.

The astronomical zeal of the Babylonians was in general, it must be confessed, no simple and pure love of an abstract science. A school of pure astronomers existed among them; but the bulk of those who engaged in the study undoubtedly pursued it in the belief that the heavenly bodies had a mysterious influence, not only upon the seasons, but upon the lives and actions of men-an influence which it was possible to discover and to foretell by prolonged and careful observation. The ancient writers, Biblical and other, state this fact in the strongest way; and the extant astronomical remains distinctly confirm it. The great majority of the tablets are of an astrological character, recording the supposed influence of the heavenly bodies, singly, in conjunction, or in opposition, upon all sublunary affairs, from the fate of empires to the washing of hands or the paring of nails. The modern prophetical almanac is the legitimate descendant and the sufficient representative of the ancient Chaldee Ephemeris, which was just as silly, just as pretentious, and just as worthless.

The Chaldee astrology was, primarily and mainly, genethlialogical. It inquired under what aspect of the heavens persons were born, or conceived, and, from the position of the celestial bodies at one or other of these moments, it professed to deduce the whole life and fortunes of the individual. According to Diodorus, it was believed that a particular star or constellation presided over the birth of each person, and thenceforward exercised over his life a special malign or benignant influence. But his lot depended, not on this star alone, but on the entire aspect of the heavens at a certain moment. To cast the horoscope was to reproduce this aspect, and then to read by means of it the individual's future.

Chaldee astrology, was not, however, limited to genethlialogy. The Chaldaeans professed to predict from the stars such things as the changes of the weather, high winds and storms, great heats, the appearance of comets, eclipses, earthquakes, and the like. They published lists of luck and unlucky days, and tables showing what aspect of the heavens portended good or evil to particular countries. Curiously enough, it appears that they regarded their art as locally limited to the regions inhabited by themselves and their kinsmen, so that while they could boldly predict storm, tempest, failing or abundant crops, war, famine, and the like, for Syria, Babylonia, and Susiana, they could venture on no prophecies with respect to other neighboring lands, as Persia, Media, Armenia.

A certain amount of real meteorological knowledge was probably mixed up with the Chaldaean astrology. Their calendars, like modern almanacs, boldly predicted the weather for fixed days in the year. They must also have been mathematicians to no inconsiderable extent, since their methods appear to have been geometrical. It is said that the Greek mathematicians often quoted with approval the works of their Chaldaean predecessors, Ciden, Naburianus, and Sudinus. Of the nature and extent of their mathematical acquirements, no account, however, can be given, since the writers who mention them enter into no details on the subject.

Chapter VI. Manners and Customs

"Girded with girdles upon their loins, exceeding in dyed attire upon their heads, all of them princes to look to, after the manner of the Babylonians of Chaldaea, the land of their nativity." —Ezek. xxiii. 15.

The manners and customs of the Babylonians, though not admitting of that copious illustration from ancient monuments which was found possible in the case of Assyria, are yet sufficiently known to us, either from the extant remains or from the accounts of ancient writers of authority, to furnish materials for a short chapter. Herodotus, Strabo, Diodorus, and Nicolas of Damascus, present us with many interesting traits of this somewhat singular people; the sacred writers contemporary with the acme of the nation add numerous touches; while the remains, though scanty, put distinctly and vividly before our eyes a certain number of curious details.

Herodotus describes with some elaboration the costume of the Babylonians in his day. He tells us that they wore a long linen gown reaching down to their feet, a woollen gown or tunic above this, a short cloak or cape of a white color, and shoes like those of the Boeotians. Their hair they allowed to grow long, but confined it by a head-band or a turban; and they always carried a walking-stick with a carving of some kind on the handle. This portraiture, it is probable, applies to the richer inhabitants of the capital, and represents the Babylonian gentleman of the fifth century before our era, as he made his appearance in the streets of the metropolis.

The cylinders seem to show that the ordinary Babylonian dress was less complicated. The worshipper who brings an offering to a god is frequently represented with a bare head, and wears apparently but one garment, a tunic generally ornamented with a diagonal fringe, and reaching from the shoulder to a little above the knee.

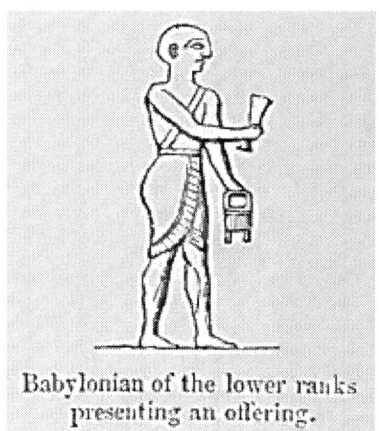

Babylonian of the lower ranks presenting an offering.

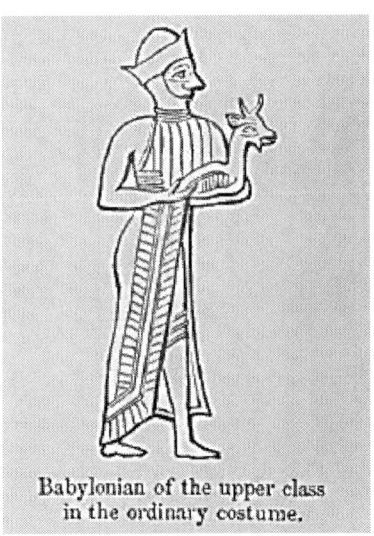

Babylonian of the upper class in the ordinary costume.

The tunic is confined round the waist by a belt. Richer worshippers, who commonly present a goat, have a fillet or headband, not a turban, round the head. They wear generally the same sort of tunic as the others; but over it they have a long robe, shaped like a modern dressing-gown, except that it has no sleeves, and does not cover the right shoulder. In a few instances only we see underneath this open gown a long inner dress or robe, such as that described by Herodotus. A cape or tippet of the kind which he describes is worn sometimes by a god, but is never seen, it is believed, in any representation of a mortal.

The short tunic, worn by the poorer worshippers, is seen also in a representation (hereafter to be given) of hunters attacking a lion.

Babylonian wearing a long under garment.

A similar garment is worn by the man-probably a slave-who accompanies the dog, supposed to represent an Indian hound; and also by a warrior, who appears on one of the cylinders conducting six foreign captives. There is consequently much reason to believe that such a tunic formed the ordinary costume of the common people, as it does at present of the common Arab inhabitants of the country. It left the arms and right shoulder bare, covering only the left. Below the belt it was not made like a frock but lapped over in front, being in fact not so much a garment as a piece of cloth wrapped round the body. Occasionally it is represented as patterned; but this is somewhat unusual.

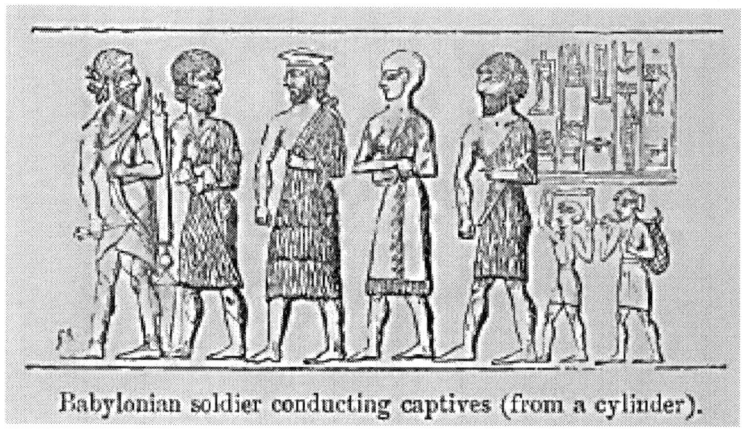

Babylonian soldier conducting captives (from a cylinder).

In lieu of the long robe reaching to the feet, which seems to have been the ordinary costume of the higher classes, we observe sometimes a shorter, but still a similar garment —a sort of coat without sleeves, fringed down both sides, and reaching only a little below the knee. The worshippers who wear this robe have in most cases the head adorned with a fillet.

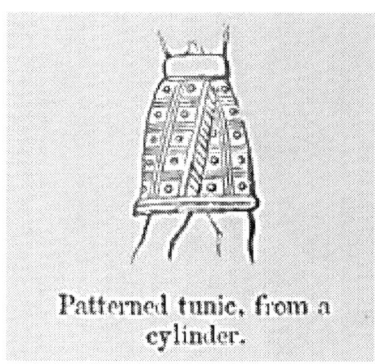

Patterned tunic, from a cylinder.

It is unusual to find any trace of boots or shoes in the representations of Babylonians. A shoe patterned with a sort of check work was worn by the king; and soldiers seem to have worn a low boot in their expeditions. But with rare exceptions the Babylonians are represented with bare feet on the monuments; and if they commonly wore shoes in the time of Herodotus, we may conjecture that they had adopted the practice from the example of the Medes and Persians. A low boot, laced in front, was worn by the chiefs of the Susianians. Perhaps the "peculiar shoe" of the Babylonians was not very different.

Babylonian wearing a short open coat.

The girdle was an essential feature of Babylonian costume, common to high and low, to the king and to the peasant. It was a broad belt, probably of leather, and encircled the waist rather high up. The warrior carried his daggers in it; to the common man it served the purpose of keeping in place the cloth which he wore round his body. According to Herodotus, it was also universal in Babylonia to carry a seal and a walking-stick.

Costume of a Susianian chief (Koyunjik).

Special costumes, differing considerably from those hitherto described, distinguished the king and the priests. The king wore a long gown, somewhat scantily made, but reaching down to the ankles, elaborately patterned and fringed. Over this, apparently, he had a close-fitting sleeved vest, which came down to the knees, and terminated in a set of heavy tassels. The girdle was worn outside the outer vest, and in war the monarch carried also two cross-belts, which perhaps supported his quiver. The upper vest was, like the under one, richly adorned with embroidery. From it, or from the girdle, depended in front a single heavy tassel attached by a cord, similar to that worn by the early kings of Assyria.

Tho tiara of the monarch was very remarkable. It was of great height, nearly cylindrical, but with a slight tendency to swell out toward the crown, which was ornamented with a row of feathers round its entire circumference. The space below was patterned with rosettes, sacred trees, and mythological figures. From the centre of the crown there rose above the feathers a projection resembling in some degree the projection which distinguishes the tiara of the Assyrian kings, the rounded, and not squared, at top. This head-dress, which has a heavy appearance, was worn low on the brow, and covered nearly all the back of the head. It can scarcely have been composed of a heaver material than cloth or felt. Probably it was brilliantly colored.

The monarch wore bracelets, but (apparently) neither necklaces nor earrings. Those last are assigned by Nicolas of Damascus to a Babylonian governor; and they were so commonly used by the Assyrians that we can scarcely suppose them unknown to their kindred and neighbors. The Babylonian monuments, however, contain no traces of earrings as worn by men, and only a few doubtful ones of collars or necklaces; whence we may at any rate conclude that neither were worn at all generally.

Costumes of the priests.

Priest wearing a peculiar mitre.

The bracelets which encircle the royal wrist resemble the most common bracelet of the Assyrians, consisting of a plain band, probably of metal, with a rosette in the centre.

The dress of the priests was a long robe or gown, flounced and striped, over which they seem to have worn an open jacket of a similar character. A long scarf or riband depended from behind down their backs. They carried on their heads an elaborate crown or mitre, which is assigned also to many of the gods. In lieu of this mitre, we find sometimes, though rarely, a horned cap; and, in one or two instances, a mitre of a different kind. In all sacrificial and ceremonial acts the priests seem to have worn their heads covered.

On the subject of the Babylonian military costume our information is scanty and imperfect. In the time of Herodotus the Chaldaeans seem to have had the same armature as the Assyrians-namely, bronze helmets, linen breastplates, shields, spears, daggers, and maces or clubs; and, at a considerably earlier date, we find in Scripture much the same arms, offensive and defensive, assigned them. There is, however, one remarkable difference between the Biblical account and that given by Herodotus. The Greek historian says nothing of the use of bows by the Chaldaeans; while in Scripture the bow appears as their favorite weapon, that which principally renders them formidable. The monuments are on this point thoroughly in accordance with Scripture. The Babylonian king already represented carries a bow and two arrows. The soldier conducting captives has a bow an arrow, and a quiver. A monument of an earlier date, which is perhaps rather Proto-Chaldaean than pure Babylonian, yet which has certain Babylonian characteristics, makes the arms of a king a bow and arrow, a club (?), and a dagger. In the marsh fights of the Assyrians, where their enemies are probably Chaldaeans of the low country, the bow is the sole weapon which we see in use.

Priest-Vizier presenting captives to a king.

The Babylonian bow nearly resembles the ordinary curved bow of the Assyrians. It has a knob at either extremity, over which the string passes, and is thicker towards the middle than at the two ends; the bend is slight, the length when strung less than four feet. The length of the arrow is about three feet.

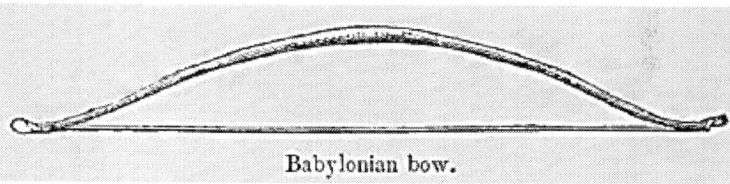

Babylonian bow.

It is carefully notched and feathered, and has a barbed point. The quiver, as represented in the Assyrian sculptures, has nothing remarkable about it; but the single extant Babylonian representation makes it terminate curiously with a large ornament resembling a spearhead. It is difficult to see the object of this appendage, which must have formed no inconsiderable addition to the weight of the quiver.

Babylonian daggers were short, and shaped like the Assyrian; but their handles were less elegant and less elaborately ornamented. They were worn in the girdle (as they are at the present day in all eastern countries) either in pairs or singly.

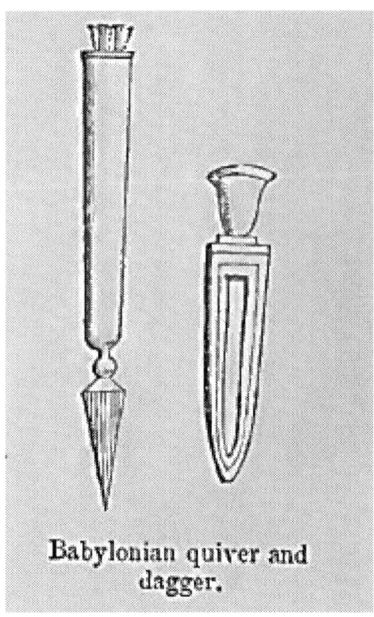

Babylonian quiver and dagger.

Other weapons of the Babylonians, which we may be sure they used in war, though the monuments do not furnish any proof of the fact, were the spear and the bill or axe. These weapons are exhibited in combination upon one of the most curious of the cylinders, where a lion is disturbed in his meal off an ox by two rustics, one of whom attacks him in front with a spear, while the other seizes his tail and assails him in the rear with an axe.

Lion attacked with spear and axe.

With the axe here represented may be compared another, which is found on a clay tablet brought from Sinkara, and supposed to belong to the early Chaldaean period.30 The Sinkara axe has a simple square blade: the axe upon the cylinder has a blade with long curved sides and a curved edge; while, to balance the weight of the blade, it has on the lower side three sharp spikes. The difference between the two implements marks the advance of mechanical art in the country between the time of the first and that of the fourth monarchy.

Axes, Chaldæan and Babylonian.

Babylonian armies seem to have been composed, like Assyrian, of three elements-infantry, cavalry, and chariots. Of the chariots we appear to have one or two representations upon the cylinders, but they are too rudely carved to be of much value. It is not likely that the chariots differed much either in shape or equipment from the Assyrian, unless they were, like those of Susiana, ordinarily drawn by mules. A peculiar car, four-wheeled, and drawn by four horses, with an elevated platform in front and a seat behind for the driver, which the cylinders occasionally exhibit, is probably not a war-chariot, but a sacred vehicle, like the tensa or thensa of the Romans.

Babylonian four-horse chariot.

The Prophet Habakkuk evidently considered the cavalry of the Babylonians to be their most formidable arm. "They are terrible and dreadful," he said; "from them shall proceed judgment and captivity; their horses also are swifter than the leopards, and are more fierce than the evening wolves; and their horsemen shall spread themselves, and their horsemen shall come from far; they shall fly, as the eagle that hasteth to eat." Similarly Ezekiel spoke of the "desirable young men, captains and rulers, great lords and renowned; all of them riding upon horses," Jeremiah couples the horses with the chariots, as if he doubted whether the chariot force or the cavalry were the more to be dreaded. "Behold, he shall come up as clouds, and his chariot shall be as a whirlwind; his horses are swifter than eagles. Woe unto us! for we are spoiled." In the army of Xerxes the Babylonians seem to have served only on foot, which would imply that they were not considered in that king's time to furnish such good cavalry as the Persians, Medes, Cissians, Indians, and others, who sent contingents of horse. Darius, however, in the Behistun inscription, speaks of Babylonian horsemen; and the armies which overran Syria, Palestine, and

Egypt, seem to have consisted mainly of horse. The Babylonian armies, like the Persian, were vast hosts, poorly disciplined, composed not only of native troops, but of contingents from the subject nations, Cissians, Elamites, Shuhites, Assyrians, and others. They marched with vast noise and tumult, spreading themselves far and wide over the country which they were invading, plundering and destroying on all sides. If their enemy would consent to a pitched battle, they were glad to engage with him; but, more usually, their contests resolved themselves into a succession of sieges, the bulk of the population attacked retreating to their strongholds, and offering behind walls a more or less protracted resistance. The weaker towns were assaulted with battering-rams; against the stronger, mounds were raised, reaching nearly to the top of the walls, which were then easily scaled or broken down. A determined persistence in sieges seems to have characterized this people, who did not take Jerusalem till the third, nor Tyre till the fourteenth year.

In expeditions it sometimes happened that a question arose as to the people or country next to be attacked. In such cases it appears that recourse was had to divination, and the omens which were obtained decided whither the next effort of the invader should be directed. Priests doubtless accompanied the expeditions to superintend the sacrifices and interpret them on such occasions. According to Diodorus, the priests in Babylonia were a caste, devoted to the service of the native deities and the pursuits of philosophy, and held in high honor by the people. It was their business to guard the temples and serve at the altars of the gods, to explain dreams and prodigies, to understand omens, to read the warnings of the stars, and to instruct men how to escape the evils threatened in those various ways, by purifications, incantations, and sacrifices. They possessed a traditional knowledge which had come down from father to son, and which none thought of questioning. The laity looked up to them as the sole possessors of a recondite wisdom of the last importance to humanity.

With these statements of the lively but inaccurate Sicilian those of the Book of Daniel are very fairly, if not entirely, in accordance. A class of "wise men" is described as existing at Babylon, foremost among whom are the Chaldaeans; they have a special "learning," and (as it would seem) a special "tongue;" their business is to expound dreams and prodigies; they are in high favor with the monarch, and are often consulted by him. This body of "wise men" is subdivided into four classes —"Chaldaeans, magicians, astrologers, and soothsayers" —a subdivision which seems to be based upon difference of occupation. It is not distinctly stated that they are priests; nor does it seem that they were a caste; for Jews are enrolled among their number, and Daniel himself is made chief of the entire body. But they form a very distinct order, and constitute a considerable power in the state; they have direct communication with the monarch, and they are believed to possess, not merely human learning, but a supernatural power of predicting future events. High civil office is enjoyed by some of their number.

Notices agreeing with these, but of less importance, are contained in Herodotus and Strabo. Herodotus speaks of the Chaldaeans as "priests;" Strabo says that they were "philosophers," who occupied themselves principally in astronomy. The latter writer mentions that they were divided into sects, who differed one from another in their doctrines. He gives the names of several Chaldaeans whom the Greek mathematicians were in the habit of quoting. Among them is a Seleucus, who by his name should be a Greek.

From these various authorities we may assume that there was in Babylon, as in Egypt, and in later Persia, a distinct priest class, which enjoyed high consideration. It was not, strictly speaking, a caste. Priests may have generally brought up their sons to the occupation; but other persons, even foreigners (and if foreigners, then *a fortiori* natives), could be enrolled in the order, and attain its highest privileges. It was at once a sacerdotal and a learned body. It had a literature, written in peculiar language, which its members were bound to study. This language and this literature were probably a legacy from the old times of the first (Turano-Cushite) kingdom, since even in Assyria it is found that the literature was in the main Turanian, down to the very close of the empire. Astronomy, astrology, and mythology were no doubt the chief subjects which the priests studied; but history, chronology, grammar, law, and natural science most likely occupied some part of their attention. Conducting everywhere the worship of the gods, they were of course scattered far and wide through the country; but they had certain special seats of learning, corresponding perhaps in some sort to our universities, the most famous of which were Erech or Orchoe (Warka), and Borsippa, the town represented by the modern Birs-i-Nimrud. They were diligent students, not wanting in ingenuity, and not content merely to hand down the wisdom of their ancestors. Schools arose among them; and a boldness of speculation developed itself akin to that which we find among the Greeks. Astronomy, in particular, was cultivated with a good deal of success; and stores were accumulated of which the Greeks in later times understood and acknowledged the value.

In social position the priest class stood high. They had access to the monarch: they were feared and respected by the people; the offerings of the faithful made them wealthy; their position as interpreters of the divine will secured them influence. Being regarded as capable of civil employment, they naturally enough obtained frequently important offices, which added to their wealth and consideration.

The mass of the people in Babylonia were employed in the two pursuits of commerce and agriculture. The commerce was both foreign and domestic. Great numbers of the Babylonians were engaged in the manufacture of those textile fabrics, particularly carpets and muslins, which Babylonia produced not only for her own use, but also for the consumption of foreign countries. Many more must have been employed as lapidaries in the execution of those delicate engravings on hard stone, wherewith the seal, which every Babylonian carried, was as a matter of course adorned. The ordinary trades and handicrafts practised in the East no doubt flourished in the country. A brisk import and export trade was constantly kept up, and promoted a healthful activity throughout the entire body politic. Babylonia is called "a land of traffic" by Ezekiel, and Babylon "a city of merchants." Isaiah says "theory of the Chaldaeans" was "in their ships." The monuments show that from very early times the people of the low country on the borders of the Persian Gulf were addicted to maritime pursuits, and navigated the gulf freely, if they did not even venture on the open ocean. And AEschylus is a witness that the nautical character still attached to the people after their conquest by the Persians; for he calls the Babylonians in the army of Xerxes "navigators of ships."

The Babylonian import trade, so far as it was carried on by themselves, seems to have been chiefly with Arabia, with the islands in the Persian Gulf, and directly or indirectly with India. From Arabia they must have imported the frankincense which they used largely in their religious ceremonies; from the Persian Gulf they appear to have derived pearls, cotton, and wood for walking sticks from India they obtained dogs and several kinds of gems. If we may believe Strabo, they had a colony called Gerrha, most favorably situated on the Arabian coast of the gulf, which was a great emporium, and conducted not only the trade between Babylonia and the regions to the south, but also that which passed through Babylonia into the more nothern districts. The products of the various countries of Western Asia flowed into Babylonia down the courses of the rivers. From Armenia, or rather Upper Mesopotamia, came wine, gems, emery, and perhaps stone for building; from Phoenicia, by way of Palmyra and Thapsacus, came tin, perhaps copper, probably musical instruments, and other objects of luxury; from Media and the countries towards the east came fine wool, lapis-lazuli, perhaps silk, and probably gold and ivory. But these imports seem to have been brought to Babylonia by foreign merchants rather than imported by the exertions of native traders. The Armenians, the Phoenicians, and perhaps the Greeks, used for the conveyance of their goods the route of the Euphrates. The Assyrians, the Parataceni, and the Medes probably floated theirs down the Tigris and its tributaries.

A large-probably the largest-portion of the people must have been engaged in the occupations of agriculture. Babylonia was, before all things, a grain-producing country-noted for a fertility unexampled elsewhere, and to moderns almost incredible. The soil was a deep and rich alluvium, and was cultivated with the utmost care. It grew chiefly wheat, barley millet, and sesame, which all nourished with wonderful luxuriance. By a skilful management of the natural water supply, the indispensable fluid was utilized to the utmost, and conveyed to every part of the country. Date-groves spread widely over the land, and produced abundance of an excellent fruit.

For the cultivation of the date nothing was needed but a proper water supply, and a little attention at the time of fructification. The male and female palm are distinct trees, and the female cannot produce fruit unless the pollen from the male comes in contact with its blossoms. If the male and the female trees are grown in proper proximity, natural causes will always produce a certain amount of impregnation. But to obtain a good crop, art may be serviceably applied. According to Herodotus, the Babylonians were accustomed to tie the branches of the male to those of the female palm. This was doubtless done at the blossoming time, when it would have the effect he mentions, preventing the fruit of the female, or date-producing palms, from falling off.

The date palm was multiplied in Babylonia by artificial means. It was commonly grown from seed, several stones being planted together for greater security; But occasionally it was raised from suckers or cuttings. It was important to plant the seeds and cuttings in a sandy soil; and if nature had not sufficiently impregnated the ground with saline particles, salt had to be applied artificially to the soil around as a dressing. The young plants needed a good deal of attention. Plentiful watering was required; and transplantation was desirable at the end of both the first and second year. The Babylonians are said to have transplanted their young trees in the height of summer; other nations preferred the springtime.

For the cultivation of grain the Babylonians broke up their land with the plough; to draw which they seem to have employed two oxen, placed one before the other, in the mode still common in many parts of England. The plough had two handles, which the ploughman guided with his two hands. It was apparently of somewhat slight construction. The tail rose from the lower part of one of the handles, and was of unusual length.

Men ploughing, from a cylinder.

It is certain that dates formed the main food of the inhabitants, The dried fruit, being to them the staff of life, was regarded by the Greeks as their "bread." It was perhaps pressed into cakes, as is the common practice in the country at the present day. On this and goat's milk, which we know to have been in use, the poorer class, it is probable, almost entirely subsisted.

Milking the goat, from a cylinder.

Palm-wine, the fermented sap of the tree, was an esteemed, but no doubt only an occasional beverage. It was pleasant to the taste, but apt to leave a headache behind it. Such vegetables as gourds, melons, and cucumbers, must have been cheap, and may have entered into the diet of the common people. They were also probably the consumers of the "pickled bats," which (according to Strabo) were eaten by the Babylonians.

In the marshy regions of the south there were certain tribes whose sole, or at any rate whose chief, food was fish. Fish abound in these districts, and are readily taken either with the hook or in nets. The mode of preparing this food was to dry it in the sun, to pound it fine, strain it through a sieve, and then make it up into cakes, or into a kind of bread.

The diet of the richer classes was no doubt varied and luxurious. Wheaten bread, meats of various kinds, luscious fruits, fish, game, loaded the board; and wine, imported from abroad was the usual beverage. The wealthy Babylonians were fond of drinking to excess; their banquets were magnificent, but generally ended in drunkenness; they were not, however, mere scenes of coarse indulgence, but had a certain refinement, which distinguishes them from the riotous drinking-bouts of the less civilized Modes. Music was in Babylonia a recognized accompaniment of the feast; and bands of performers, entering with the wine, entertained the guests with concerted pieces. A rich odor of perfume floated around, for the Babylonians were connoisseurs in unguents. The eye was delighted with a display of gold and silver plate. The splendid dresses of the guests, the exquisite carpets and hangings, the numerous attendants, gave an air of grandeur to the scene, and seemed half to excuse the excess of which too many were guilty.

A love of music appears to have characterized both the Babylonians and their near neighbors and kinsmen, the Susianians. In the sculptured representations of Assyria, the Susianians are shown to have possessed numerous instruments, and to have organized large bands of performers. The Prophet Daniel and the historian Ctesias similarly witness to the musical taste of the Babylonians, which had much the same character. Ctesias said that Annarus (or Nannarus), a Babylonian noble, entertained his guests at a banquet with music performed by a company of 150 women. Of these a part sang, while the rest played upon instruments, some using the pipe, others the harp, and a certain number the psaltery. These same instruments are assigned to the Babylonians by the prophet Daniel, who, however, adds to them three more–viz., the horn, the sambuca, and an instrument called the sumphonia, or "symphony." It is uncertain whether the horn intended was straight, like the Assyrian, or curved, like the Roman cornu and lituus. The pipe was probably the double instrument, played at the end, which was familiar to the Susianians and Assyrians. The harp would seem to have resembled the later harp of the Assyrians; but it had fewer strings, if we may judge from a representation upon a cylinder. Like the Assyrian, it was carried under one arm, and was played by both hands, one on either side of the strings.

Babylonian harp, from a cylinder.

The character of the remaining instruments is more doubtful. The sambuca seems to have been a large harp, which rested on the ground, like the harps of the Egyptians. The psaltery was also a stringed instrument, and, if its legitimate descendant is the modern santour, we may presume that it is represented in the hands of a Susianian musician on the monument which is our chief authority for the Oriental music of the period. The symphonia is thought by some to be the bagpipe, which is called sampogna by the modern Italians: by others it is regarded as a sort of organ.

The Babylonians used music, not merely in their private entertainments, but also in their religious ceremonies. Daniel's account of their instruments occurs casually in his mention of Nebuchadnezzar's dedication of a colossal idol of gold. The worshippers were to prostrate themselves before the idol as soon as they heard the music commence, and were probably to continue in the attitude of worship until the sound ceased.

The seclusion of women seems scarcely to have been practised in Babylonia with as much strictness as in most Oriental countries. The two peculiar customs on which Herodotus descants at length-the public auction of the marriageable virgins in all the towns of the empire, and the religious prostitution authorized in the worship of Beltis-were wholly incompatible with the restraints to which the sex has commonly submitted in the Eastern world. Much modesty can scarcely have belonged to those whose virgin charms were originally offered in the public market to the best bidder, and who were required by their religion, at least once in their lives, openly to submit to the embraces of a man other than their husband. It would certainly seem that the sex had in Babylonia a freedom-and not only a freedom, but also a consideration-unusual in the ancient world, and especially rare in Asia. The stories of Semiramis and Nitocris may have in them no great amount of truth; but they sufficiently indicate the belief of the Greeks as to the comparative publicity allowed to their women by the Babylonians.

The monuments accord with the view of Babylonian manners thus opened to us. The female form is not eschewed by the Chaldaean artists. Besides images of a goddess (Beltis or Ish-tar) suckling a child, which are frequent, we find on the cylinders numerous representations of women, engaged in various employments.

Babylonian women making an offering to a goddess.

Sometimes they are represented in a procession, visiting the shrine of a goddess, to whom they offer their petitions, by the mouth of one of their number, or to whom they bring their children for the purpose, probably, of placing them under her protection, sometimes they may be seen amusing themselves among birds and flowers in a garden, plucking the fruit from dwarf palms, and politely handing it to one another. Their attire is in every case nearly the same; they wear a long but scanty robe, reaching to the ankles, ornamented at the bottom with a fringe and apparently opening in front. The upper part of the dress passes over only one shoulder. It is trimmed round the top with a fringe which runs diagonally across the chest, and a similar fringe edges the dress down the front where it opens.

Babylonian women gathering dates in a garden.

A band or fillet is worn round the head, confining the hair, which is turned back behind the head, and tied by a riband, or else held up by the fillet.

Female ornaments are not perceptible on the small figures of the cylinders; but from the modelled image in clay, of which a representation has been already given, we learn that bracelets and earrings of a simple character were worn by Babylonian women, if they were not by the men. On the whole, however, female dress seems to have been plain and wanting in variety, though we may perhaps suspect that the artists do not trouble themselves to represent very accurately such diversities of apparel as actually existed.

From a single representation of a priestess it would seem that women of that class wore nothing but a petticoat, thus exposing not only the arms, but the whole of the body as far as the waist.

The monuments throw a little further light on the daily life of the Babylonians. A few of their implements, as saws and hatchets, are represented; and from the stools, the chairs, the tables, and stands for holding water-jars which occur occasionally on the cylinders, we may gather that the fashion of their furniture much resembled that of their northern neighbors, the Assyrians. It is needless to dwell on this subject, which presents no novel features, and has been anticipated by the discussion on Assyrian furniture in the first volume. The only touch that can be added to what was there said is that in Babylonia, the chief-almost the sole-material employed for furniture was the wood of the palm-tree, a soft and light fabric which could be easily worked, and which had considerable strength, but did not admit of a high finish.

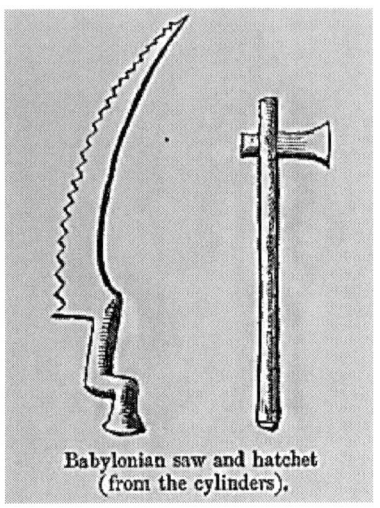

Babylonian saw and hatchet
(from the cylinders).

Chapter VII. Religion

The Religion of the later Babylonians differed in so few respects from that of the early Chaldaeans, their predecessors in the same country, that it will be unnecessary to detain the reader with many observations on the subject. The same gods were worshipped in the same temples and with the same rites-the same cosmogony was taught and held-the same symbols were objects of religious regard-even the very dress of the priests was maintained unaltered; and, could Urukh or Chedorlaomer have risen from the grave and revisited the shrines wherein they sacrificed fourteen centuries earlier, they would have found but little to distinguish the ceremonies of their own day from those in vogue under the successors of Nabopolassar. Some additional splendor in the buildings, the idols, and perhaps the offerings, some increased use of music as a part of the ceremonial, some advance of corruption with respect to priestly impostures and popular religious customs might probably have been noticed; but otherwise the religion of Nabonidus and Belshazzar was that of Urukh and Ilgi, alike in the objects and the mode of worship, in the theological notions entertained and the ceremonial observances taught and practised.

The identity of the gods worshipped during the entire period is sufficiently proved by the repair and restoration of the ancient temples under Nebuchadnezzar, and their re-dedication (as a general rule) to the same deities. It appears also from the names of the later kings and nobles, which embrace among their elements the old divine appellations. Still, together with this general uniformity, we seem to see a certain amount of fluctuation —a sort of fashion in the religion, whereby particular gods were at different times exalted to a higher rank in the Pantheon, and were sometimes even confounded with other deities commonly regarded as wholly distinct from them. Thus Nebuchadnezzar devoted himself in an especial way to Merodach, and not only assigned him titles of honor which implied his supremacy over all the remaining gods, but even identified him with the great Bel, the ancient tutelary god of the capital. Nabonidus, on the other hand, seems to have restored Bel to his old position, re-establishing the distinction between him and Merodach, and preferring to devote himself to the former.

A similar confusion occurs between the goddesses Beltis and Nana or Ishtar, though this is not peculiar to the later kingdom. It may perhaps be suspected from such instances of connection and quasi-convertibility, that an esoteric doctrine, known to the priests and communicated by them to the kings, taught the real identity of the several gods and goddesses, who may have been understood by the better instructed to represent, not distinct and separate beings, but the several phases of the Divine Nature. Ancient polytheism had, it may be surmised, to a great extent this origin, the various names and titles of the Supreme, which designated His different attributes or the different spheres of His operation, coming by degrees to be misunderstood, and to pass, first with the vulgar, and at last with all but the most enlightened, for the appellations of a number of gods.

The chief objects of Babylonian worship were Bel, Merodach, and Nebo. Nebo, the special deity of Borsippa, seems to have been regarded as a sort of powerful patron-saint under whose protection it was important to place individuals. During the period of the later kingdom, no divine element is so common in names. Of the seven kings who form the entire list, three certainly, four probably, had appellations composed with it. The usage extended from the royal house to the courtiers; and such names as Nebu-zar-adan, Samgar-Nebo, and Nebushazban, show the respect which the upper class of citizens paid to this god. It may even be suspected that when Nebuchadnezzar's Master of the Eunuchs had to give Babylonian names to the young Jewish princes whom he was educating, he designed to secure for one of them this powerful patron, and consequently called him Abed-Nebo —the servant of Nebo —a name which the later Jews, either disdaining or not understanding, have corrupted into the Abed-nego of the existing text.

Another god held in peculiar honor by the Babylonians was Nergal. Worshipped at Cutha as the tutelary divinity of the town, he was also held in repute by the people generally. No name is more common on the cylinder seals. It is sometimes, though not often, an element in the names of men, as in "Nergal-shar-ezer, the Eab-mag," and (if he be a different person) in Neriglissar, the king.

Altogether, there was a strong local element in the religion of the Babylonians. Bel and Merodach were in a peculiar way the gods of Babylon, Nebo of Borsippa, Nergal of Cutha, the Moon of Ur or Hur, Beltis of Niffer, Hea or Hoa of Hit, Ana of Erech, the Sun of Sippara. Without being exclusively honored at a single site, the deities in question held the foremost place each in his own town. There especially was worship offered to them; there was the most magnificent of their shrines. Out of his own city a god was not greatly respected, unless by those who regarded him as their special personal protector.

The Babylonians worshipped their gods indirectly, through images. Each shrine had at least one idol, which was held in the most pious reverence, and was in the minds of the vulgar identified with the god. It seems to have been believed by some that the actual idol ate and drank the offerings. Others distinguished between the idol and the god, regarding the latter as only occasionally visiting the shrine where he was worshipped. Even these last, however, held gross anthropomorphic views, since they considered the god to descend from heaven in order to hold commerce with the chief priestess. Such notions were encouraged by the priests, who furnished the inner shrine in the temple of Bel with a magnificent couch and a golden table, and made the principal priestess pass the night in the shrine on certain occasions.

The images of the gods were of various materials. Some were of wood, others of stone, others again of metal; and these last were either solid or plated. The metals employed were gold, silver, brass, or rather bronze, and iron. Occasionally the metal was laid over a clay model. Sometimes images of one metal were overlaid with plates of another, as was the case with one of the great images of Bel, which was originally of silver but was coated with gold by Nebuchadnezzar.

The worship of the Babylonians appears to have been conducted with much pomp and magnificence. A description has been already given of their temples. Attached to these imposing structures was, in every case, a body of priests; to whom the conduct of the ceremonies and the custody of the treasures were intrusted. The priests were married, and lived with their wives and children, either in the sacred structure itself, or in its immediate neighborhood. They were supported either by lands belonging to the temple, or by the offerings of the faithful. These consisted in general of animals, chiefly oxen and goats; but other valuables were no doubt received when tendered. The priest always intervened between the worshipper and the deities, presenting him to them and interceding with uplifted hands on his behalf.

In the temple of Bel at Babylon, and probably in most of the other temples both there and elsewhere throughout the country, a great festival was celebrated once in the course of each year. We know little of the ceremonies with which these festivals were accompanied; but we may presume from the analogy of other nations that there were magnificent processions on these occasions, accompanied probably with music and dancing. The images of the gods were perhaps exhibited either on frames or on sacred vehicles. Numerous victims were sacrificed; and at Babylon it was customary to burn on the great altar in the precinct of Bel a thousand talents' weight of frankincense. The priests no doubt wore their most splendid dresses; the multitude was in holiday costume; the city was given up to merry-making. Everywhere banquets were held. In the palace the king entertained his lords; in private houses there was dancing and revelling. Wine was freely drunk; passion Was excited; and the day, it must be feared, too often terminated in wild orgies, wherein the sanctions of religion were claimed for the free indulgence of the worst sensual appetites. In the temples of one deity excesses of this description, instead of being confined to rare occasions, seem to have been of every-day occurrence. Each woman was required once in her life to visit a shrine of Beltis, and there remain till some stranger cast money in her lap and took her away with him. Herodotus, who seems to have visited the disgraceful scene, describes it as follows. "Many women of the wealthier sort, who are too proud to mix with the others, drive in covered carriages to the precinct, followed by a goodly train of attendants, and there take their station. But the larger number seat themselves within the holy inclosure with wreaths of string about their heads-and here there is always a great crowd, some coming and others going. Lines of cord mark out paths in all directions among the woman; and the strangers pass along them to make their choice. A women who has once taken her seat is not allowed to return home till one of the strangers throws a silver coin into her lap, and takes her with him beyond the holy ground. When he throws the coin, he says these words —'The goddess Mylitta (Beltis) prosper thee.' The silver coin may be of any size; it cannot be refused; for that is forbidden by the law, since once thrown it is sacred. The woman goes with the first man who throws her money, and rejects no one. When she has gone with him, and so satisfied the goddess, she returns home; and from that time forth no gift, however great, will prevail with her. Such of the women as are tall and beautiful are soon released; but others, who are ugly, have to stay a long time before they can fulfil the law. Some have even waited three or four years in the precinct." The demoralizing tendency of this religious prostitution can scarcely be overrated.

Notions of legal cleanliness and uncleanliness, akin to those prevalent among the Jews, are found to some extent in the religious system of the Babylonians. The consummation of the marriage rite made both the man and the woman impure, as did every subsequent act of the same kind. The impurity was communicated to any vessel that either might touch. To remove it, the pair were required first to sit down before a censer of burning incense, and then to wash themselves thoroughly. Thus only could they re-enter into the state of legal cleanness. A similar impurity attached to those who came into contact with a human corpse. The Babylonians are remarkable for the extent to which they affected symbolism in religion. In the first place they attached to each god a special mystic number, which is used as his emblem and may even stand for his name in an inscription. To the gods of the First Triad-Ami, Bel, and Hea or Hoa-were assigned respectively the numbers 60, 50, and 40; to those of the Second Triad-the Moon, the Sun and the Atmosphere-were given the other integers, 30, 20, and 10 (or perhaps six). To Beltis was attached the number 15, to Nergal 12, to Bar or Nin (apparently) 40, as to Hoa; but this is perhaps doubtful. It is probable that every god, or at any rate all the principle deities, had in a similar way some numerical emblem. Many of these are, however, as yet undiscovered.

Further, each god seems to have had one or more emblematic signs by which he could be pictorially symbolized. The cylinders are full of such forms, which are often crowded into every vacant space where room could be found for them. A certain number can be assigned definitely to particular divinities. Thus a circle, plain or crossed, designates the Sun-god, San or Shamas; a six-rayed or eight-rayed star the Sun-goddess, Gula or Anunit; a double or triple thunderbolt the Atmospheric god, Vul; a serpent probably Hoa; a naked female form Nana or Ishtar; a fish Bar or Nin-ip. But besides these assignable symbols, there are a vast number with regard to which we are still wholly in the dark. Among these may be mentioned a sort of double cross, often repeated three times, a jar or bottle, an altar, a double lozenge, one or more birds, an animal between a monkey and a jerboa, a dog, a sort of double horn, a sacred three, an ox, a bee, a spearhead. Each, apparently, represents a distinct deity; and the object of placing them upon a cylinder is to imply the devotion of the man whose seal it is to other deities besides those whose special servant he considers himself. A single cylinder sometimes contains as many as eight or ten such emblems.

The principal temples of the gods had special sacred appellations. The great temple of Bel at Babylon was known as Bit-Saggath, that of the same god at Niffer as Kharris-Nipra. that of Beltis at Warka (Erech) as Bit-Ana, that of the sun at Sippara as Bit-Parra, that of Anunit at the same place as Bit-Ulmis, that of Nebo at Borsippa as Bit-Tsida, etc. It is seldom that these names admit of explanation. They had come down apparently from the old Chaldaean times, and belonged to the ancient (Turanian) form of speech; which is still almost unintelligible. The

Babylonians themselves probably in few cases understood their meaning. They used the words simply as proper names, without regarding them as significative.

Chapter VIII. History and Chronology

Τῆς δὲ Βαβυλῶνος... πολλοί μεν κου...εγενοντο βασιλεες...οι τα τειχια τε εκεκοσμησαν και τα ιρα. - Herod i. 184.

The history of the Babylonian Empire commences with Nabopolassar, who appears to have mounted the throne in the year B.C. 625; but to understand the true character of the kingdom which he set up, its traditions and its national spirit, we must begin at a far earlier date. We must examine, in however incomplete and cursory a manner, the middle period of Babylonian history, the time of obscurity and comparative insignificance, when the country was as a general rule, subject to Assyria, or at any rate played but a secondary part in the affairs of the East. We shall thus prepare the way for our proper subject, while at the same time we shall link on the history of the Fourth to that of the First Monarchy, and obtain a second line of continuous narrative, connecting the brilliant era of Cyaxares and Nebuchadnezzar with the obscure period of the first Cushite kings.

It has been observed that the original Chaldaean monarchy lasted, under various dynasties from about B.C. 2400 to B.C. 1300, when it was destroyed by the Assyrians, who became masters of Babylonia under the first Tiglathi-Nin, and governed it for a short time from their own capital. Unable, however, to maintain this unity very long, they appear to have set up in the country an Assyrian dynasty, over which they claimed and sometimes exercised a kind of suzerainty, but which was practically independent and managed both the external and internal affairs of the kingdom at its pleasure. The first king of this dynasty concerning whom we have any information is a Nebuchadnezzar, who was contemporary with the Assyrian monarch Asshur-ris-ilim, and made two attacks upon his territories. The first of these was by the way of the Diyaleh and the outlying Zagros hills, the line taken by the great Persian military road in later times. The second was directly across the plain. If we are to believe the Assyrian historian who gives an account of the campaigns, both attacks were repulsed, and after his second failure the Babylonian monarch fled away into his own country hastily. We may perhaps suspect that a Babylonian writer would have told a different story. At any rate Asshur-ris-ilim was content to defend his own territories and did not attempt to retaliate upon his assailant. It was not till late in the reign of his son and successor, Tiglath-Pileser I., that any attempt was made to punish the Babylonians for their audacity. Then, however, that monarch invaded the southern kingdom, which had passed into the hands of a king named Merodach-iddin-akhi, probably a son of Nebuchadnezzar. After two years of fighting, in which he took Eurri-Galzu (Akkerkuf), the two Sipparas, Opis, and even Babylon itself, Tiglath-Pileser retired, satisfied apparently with his victories; but the Babylonian monarch was neither subdued nor daunted. Hanging on the rear of the retreating force, he harassed it by cutting off its baggage, and in this way he became possessed of certain Assyrian idols, which he carried away as trophies to Babylon. War continued between the two countries during the ensuing reigns of Merodach-shapik-ziri in Babylon and Asshur-bil-kala in Assyria, but with no important successes, so far as appears, on either side.

The century during which these wars took place between Assyria and Babylonia, which corresponds with the period of the later Judges in Israel, is followed by an obscure interval, during which but little is known of either country. Assyria seems to have been at this time in a state of great depression. Babylonia, it may be suspected, was flourishing; but as our knowledge of its condition comes to us almost entirely through the records of the sister country, which here fail us, we can only obtain a dim and indistinct vision of the greatness now achieved by the southern kingdom. A notice of Asshur-izir-pal's seems to imply that Babylon, during the period in question, enlarged her territories at the expense of Assyria, and another in Macrobius, makes it probable that she held communications with Egypt. Perhaps these two powers, fearing the growing strength of Assyria, united against her, and so checked for a while that development of her resources which they justly dreaded.

However, after two centuries of comparative depression, Assyria once more started forward, and Babylonia was among the first of her neighbors whom she proceeded to chastise and despoil. About the year B.C. 880 Asshur-izir-pal led an expedition to the south-east and recovered the territory which, had been occupied by the Babylonians during the period of weakness. Thirty years later, his son, the Black-Obelisk king, made the power of Assyria still more sensibly felt. Taking advantage of the circumstance that a civil war was raging in Babylonia between the legitimate monarch Merodach-sum-adin, and his young brother, he marched into the country, took a number of the towns, and having defeated and slain the pretender, was admitted into Babylon itself. From thence he proceeded to overrun Chaldaea, or the district upon the coast, which appears at this time to have been independent of Babylon, and governed by a number of petty kings. The Babylonian monarch probably admitted the suzerainty of the invader, but was not put to any tribute. The Chaldaean chiefs, however, had to submit to this indignity. The Assyrian monarch returned to his capital, having "struck terror as far as the sea." Thus Assyrian influence was once more extended over the whole of the southern country, and Babylonia resumed her position of a secondary power, dependent on the great monarchy of the north.

But she was not long allowed to retain even the shadow of an autonomous rule. In or about the year B.C. 821 the son and successor of the Black-Obelisk king, apparently without any pretext, made a fresh invasion of the country. Mero-dach-belatzu-ikm, the Babylonian monarch, boldly met him in the field, but was defeated in two pitched battles (in the latter of which he had the assistance of powerful allies) and was forced to submit to his antagonist. Babylon, it is probable, became at once an Assyrian tributary, and in this condition she remained till the troubles which came upon Assyria towards the middle of the eighth century B.C. gave an opportunity for shaking off the hated yoke. Perhaps the first successes were obtained by Pul, who, taking advantage of Assyria's weakness under Asshur-dayan III. (ab. B.C. 770), seems to have established a dominion over the Euphrates valley and Western Mesopotamia, from which he proceeded to carry his arms into Syria and Palestine. Or perhaps Pul's efforts merely, by still further weakening Assyria, paved the way for Babylon to revolt, and Nabonassar, who became king of Babylon in B.C. 747, is to be regarded as the re-establisher of her independence. In either case it is apparent that the recovery of independence was accompanied, or rapidly followed, by a disintegration of the country, which was of evil omen for its future greatness. While Nabonassar established himself at the head of affairs in Babylon, a certain Yakin, the father of Merodach-Baladan, became master of the tract upon the coast; and various princes, Nadina, Zakiru, and others, at the same time obtained governments, which they administered in their own name towards the north. The old Babylonian kingdom was broken up; and the way was prepared for that final subjugation which was ultimately affected by the Sargonids.

Still, the Babylonians seemed to have looked with complacency on this period, and they certainly made it an era from which to date their later history. Perhaps, however, they had not much choice in this matter. Nabonassar was a man of energy and determination. Bent probably on obliterating the memory of the preceding period of subjugation, he "destroyed the acts of the kings who had preceded him;" and the result was that the war of his accession became almost necessarily the era from which subsequent events had to be dated.

Nabonassar appears to have lived on friendly terms with Tiglath-Pileser, the contemporary monarch of Assyria, who early in his reign invaded the southern country, reduced several princes of the districts about Babylon to subjection, and forced Merodach-Baladan, who had succeeded his father, Yakin, in the low region, to become his tributary. No war seems to have been waged between Tiglath-Pileser and Nabonassar. The king of Babylon may have seen with satisfaction the humiliation of his immediate neighbors and rivals, and may have felt that their subjugation rather improved than weakened his own position. At any rate it tended to place him before the nation as their only hope and champion-the sole barrier which protected their country from a return of the old servitude.

Nabonassar held the throne of Babylon for fourteen years, from B.C. 747 to B.C. 733. It has generally been supposed that this period is the same with that regarded by Herodotus as constituting the reign of Semiramis. As the wife or as the mother of Nabonassar, that lady (according to many) directed the affairs of the Babylonian state on behalf of her husband or her son. The theory is not devoid of a certain plausibility, and it is no doubt possible that it may be true; but at present it is a mere conjecture, wholly unconfirmed by the native records; and we may question whether on the whole it is not more probable that the Semiramis of Herodotus is misplaced. In a former volume it was shown that a Semiramis flourished in Assyria towards the end of the ninth and the beginning of the eighth centuries B.C. —-during the period, that is, of Babylonian subjection to Assyria. She may have been a Babylonian princess, and have exercised an authority in the southern capital. It would seem therefore to be more probable that she is the individual whom Herodotus intends, though he has placed her about half a century too late, than that there were two persons of the same name within so short a time, both queens, and both ruling in Mesopotamia.

Nabonassar was succeeded in the year B.C. 733 by a certain Nadius, who is suspected to have been among the independent princes reduced to subjection by Tiglath-Pileser in his Babylonian expedition. Nadius reigned only two years-from B.C. 733 to B.C. 731 —when he was succeeded by Ghinzinus and Porus, two princes whose joint rule lasted from B.C. 731 to B.C. 726. They were followed by an Elulseus, who has been identified with the king of that name called by Menander king of Tyre-the Luliya of the cuneiform inscriptions; but it is in the highest degree improbable that one and the same monarch should have borne sway both in Phoenicia and Chaldaea at a time when Assyria was paramount over the whole of the intervening country. Elulseus therefore must be assigned to the same class of utterly obscure monarchs with his predecessors, Porus, Chinzinus, and Nadius; and it is only with Merodach-Baladan, his successor, that the darkness becomes a little dispelled, and we once more see the Babylonian throne occupied by a prince of some reputation and indeed celebrity.

Merodach-Baladan was the son of a monarch, who in the troublous times that preceded, or closely followed, the era of Nabonassar appears to have made himself master of the lower Babylonian territory-the true Chaldaea-and to have there founded a capital city, which he called after his own name, Bit-Yakin. On the death of his father Merodach-Baladan inherited this dominion; and it is here that we first find him, when, during the reign of Nabonassar, the Assyrians under Tiglath-Pileser II. invade the country. Forced to accept the position of Assyrian tributary under this monarch, to whom he probably looked for protection against the Babylonian king, Nabonassar, Merodach-Baladan patiently bided his time, remaining in comparative obscurity during the two reigns of Tiglath-Pileser and Shalmaneser his successor, and only emerging contemporaneously with the troubles which ushered in the dynasty of the Sargonids. In B.C. 721 —the year in which Sargon made himself master of Nineveh-Merodach-Baladan extended his authority over the upper country, and was recognized as king of Babylon. Here he maintained himself for twelve years; and it was probably at some point of time within this space that he sent embassadors to Hezekiah at Jerusalem, with orders to inquire into the particulars of the curious astronomical marvel, or miracle, which had accompanied the sickness and recovery of that monarch. It is not unlikely that the embassy, whereof this was the pretext, had a further political object. Morodach-Baladan, aware of his inability to withstand singly the forces of Assyria, was probably anxious to form a powerful league against the conquering state, which threatened to absorb the whole of Western Asia into its dominion. Hezekiah received his advances favorably, as appears by the fact that he exhibited to him all his treasures. Egypt, we may presume, was cognizant of the proceedings, and gave them her support. An alliance, defensive if not also offensive, was probably concluded between Egypt and Judaea on the one hand, Babylon, Susiana, and the Aramaean tribes of the middle Euphrates on the other. The league would have been formidable but for one circumstance-Assyria lay midway between the allied states, and could attack either moiety of the confederates separately at her pleasure. And the Assyrian king was not slow to take advantage of his situation. In two successive years Sargon marched his troops against Egypt and against Babylonia, and in both directions carried all before him. In Egypt he forced Sabaco to sue for peace. In Babylonia (B.C. 710) he gained a great victory over Merodach-Baladan and his allies, the Aramaeans and Susianians, took Bit-Yakin, into which the defeated monarch had thrown himself, and gained possession of his treasures and his person. Upon this the whole country submitted; Merodach-Baladan was carried away captive into Assyria; and Sargon himself, mounting the throne, assumed the title-rarely taken by an Assyrian monarch of "King of Babylon."

But this state of things did not continue long. Sargon died in the year B.C. 704, and co-incident with his death we find a renewal of troubles in Babylonia. Assyria's yoke was shaken off; various pretenders started up; a son of Sargon and brother of Sennacherib re-established Assyrian influence for a brief space; but fresh revolts followed. A certain Hagisa became king of Babylon for a month. Finally, Merodach-Baladan, again appeared upon the scene, having escaped from his Assyrian prison, murdered Hagisa, and remounted the throne from which he had been deposed seven years previously. But the brave effort to recover independence failed. Sennacherib in his second year, B.C. 703, descended upon Babylonia, defeated the army which Merodach-Baladan brought against him, drove that monarch himself into exile, after a reign of six months, and re-attached his country to the Assyrian crown. From this time to the revolt of Nabopolassar —a period of above three quarters of a century-Babylonia with few and brief intervals of revolt, continued an Assyrian fief. The assyrian kings governed her either by means of viceroys, such as Belibus, Regibelus, Mesesimordachus, and Saos-duchinus, or directly in their own persons, as was the case during the reign of Esarhaddon, and during the later years of Asshur-bani-pal.

The revolts of Babylon during this period have been described at length in the history of Assyria. Two fall into the reign of Sennacherib, one into that of Asshur-bani-pal, his grandson. In the former, Merodach-Baladan, who had not yet given up his pretensions to the lower country, and a certain Susub, who was acknowledged as king at Babylon, were the leaders. In the latter, Saos-duchinus, the Assyrian viceroy, and brother of Asshur-bani-pal, the Assyrian king, seduced from his allegiance by the hope of making himself independent headed the insurrection. In each case the struggle was brief, being begun and ended within the year. The power of Assyria at this time so vastly preponderated over that of her ancient rival that a single campaign sufficed on each occasion of revolt to crush the nascent insurrection.

A tabular view of the chronology of this period is appended.

Having thus briefly sketched the history of the kingdom of Babylon from its conquest by Tiglathi-Nin to the close of the long period of Assyrian predominance in Western Asia, we may proceed to the consideration of the "Empire." And first, as to the circumstances of its foundation.

When the Medes first assumed an aggressive attitude towards Assyria, and threatened the capital with a siege, Babylonia apparently remained unshaken in her allegiance. When the Scythian hordes spread themselves over Upper Mesopotamia and wasted with fire and sword the fairest regions under Assyrian rule, there was still no defection in this quarter. It was not till the Scythic ravages were over, and the Medes for the second time poured across Zagros into Adiabene, resuming the enterprise from which they had desisted at the time of the Scythic invasion, that the fidelity of the Southern people wavered. Simultaneously with the advance of the Medes against the Assyrian capital from the east, we hear of a force threatening it from the south, a force which can only have consisted of Susianians, of Babylonians, or of both combined. It is probable that the emissaries of Cyaxares had been busy in this region for some time before his second attack took place, and that by a concerted plan while the Medes debouched from the Zagros passes, the south rose in revolt and sent its hasty levies along the valley of the Tigris.

CHRONOLOGY OF BABYLON FROM THE ARAB CONQUEST TO NABOPOLASSAR.

B.C.	Kings.	Contemporary kings of Assyria.	Remarkable events.
1518 to 1273	Dynasty of Arabs	Bel-sumili-kapi. * * * Bel-lush. Pud-il. Iva-lush I. Shalmaneser I.	
1273 ab. 1273	Dynasty of Assyrians	Tiglathi-Nin I. Iva-lush II. * * * Nin-pala-zira. Asshur-dah-il. Mutaggil-Nebo.	Babylon conquered by the Assyrians.
ab. 1150	Nebuchadnezzar I.	Asshur-ris-ilim	} Wars between Assyria and Babylon.
" 1130	Merodach-iddin-akhi.	Tiglath-pileser I. ?	
" 1110	Merodach-shapik-ziri	Asshur bil-kala * * *	
	Tsibir (Deboras)	Asshur-Mazur * * * Asshur-iddin-akhi. Asshur-danin-il I. Iva-lush III. Tiglathi-Nin II.	Babylon in alliance with Egypt. Takes territory from Assyria.
ab. 880	* * *	Asshur-idanni-pal	{ Assyria recovers her lost territory.
" 850	Merodach-sum-adin	Shalmaneser II.	{ Civil war in Babylon. Assyria helps the legitimate king.
" 820	Merodach-belatzu-ikbi * * *	Shamas-Iva Iva-lush IV. Shalmaneser III. Asshur-danil-il II.	Babylon conquered. Passes under Assyria.
747	Nabonassar	Asshur-lush	{ Babylon re-establishes her independence.
744		Tiglath-pileser II.	
733	Nadius.		
731	Chinzinus and Porus		
726	Elulæus	Shalmaneser IV.	
721	Merodach-Baladan	Sargon.	
713(?)			{ Embassy of Merodach-Baladan to Hezekiah.
709	Arceanus (viceroy)		Babylon conquered by Sargon.
704	Interregnum	Sennacherib	Babylon revolts.
703	{ Hagisa { Merodach-Baladan }		Sennacherib conquers Babylon.
702	Belibus (viceroy).		
699	Assaranadius (viceroy).		
696(?)	Susub		{ Babylon revolts. Revolt put down.
694(?)			Ditto.
693	Regibelus (viceroy).		
692	Mesesimordachus (viceroy).		
688	Interregnum		{ Troubles in Babylon. Interregnum of eight years, coinciding with last eight years of Sennacherib.
680	Esarhaddon	Esarhaddon	{ Babylon recovered by Esarhaddon.
667	Saos-duchinus (viceroy)	Asshur-bani-pal	{ Babylon revolts and again returns to allegiance.
647	Cinneladanus	Asshur-emit-ilin.	
625	Nabopolassar		Assyrian empire destroyed.

In this strait the Assyrian king deemed it necessary to divide his forces and to send a portion against the enemy which was advancing from the south, while with the remainder he himself awaited the coming of the Medes. The troops detached for the former service he placed under the command of a certain Nabopolassar? (Nabu-pal-uzur), who was probably an Assyrian nobleman of high rank and known capacity. Nabopolassar had orders to proceed to Babylon, of which he was probably made viceroy, and to defend the southern capital against the rebels. We may conclude that he obeyed these orders so far as to enter Babylon and install himself in office; but shortly afterwards he seems to have made up his mind to break faith with his sovereign, and aim at obtaining for himself an independent kingdom out of the ruins of the Assyrian power. Having formed this resolve, his first step was to send an embassy to Cyaxares, and to propose terms of alliance, while at the same time he arranged a marriage between his own son, Nebuchadnezzar, and Amuhia, or Amyitis (for the name is written both ways), the daughter of the Median monarch.

Cyaxares gladly accepted the terms offered; the young persons were betrothed; and Nabopolassar immediately led, or sent, a contingent of troops to join the Medes, who took an active part in the great siege which resulted in the capture and destruction of the Assyrian capital.

A division of the Assyrian Empire between the allied monarchs followed. While Cyaxares claimed for his own share Assyria Proper and the various countries dependent on Assyria towards the north and the north-west, Nabopolassar was rewarded by his timely defection, not merely by independence but by the transfer to his government of Susiana on the one hand and of the valley of the Euphrates, Syria, and Palestine on the other. The transfer appears to have been effected quietly, the Babylonian yoke being peacefully accepted in lieu of the Assyrian without the necessity arising for any application of force. Probably it appeared to the subjects of Assyria, who had been accustomed to a monarch holding his court alternately at Nineveh and at Babylon, that the new power was merely a continuation of the old, and the monarch a legitimate successor of the old line of Ninevite kings.

Of the reign of Nabopolassar the information which has come down to us is scanty. It appears by the canon of Ptolemy that he dated his accession to the throne from the year B.C. 625, and that his reign lasted twenty-one years, from B.C. 625 to B.C. 604. During the greater portion of this period the history of Babylon is a blank. Apparently the "golden city" enjoyed her new position at the head of an empire too much to endanger it by aggression; and, her peaceful attitude provoking no hostility, she was for a while left unmolested by her neighbors. Media, bound to her by formal treaty as well as by dynastic interests, could be relied upon as a firm friend; Persia was too weak, Lydia too remote, to be formidable; in Egypt alone was there a combination of hostile feeling with military strength such as might have been expected to lead speedily to a trial of strength; but Egypt was under the rule of an aged and wary prince, one trained in the school of adversity, whose years forbade his engaging in any distant enterprise, and whose prudence led him to think more of defending his own country than of attacking others. Thus, while Psammetichus lived, Babylon had little to fear from any quarter, and could afford to "give herself to pleasures and dwell carelessly."

The only exertion which she seems to have been called upon to make during her first eighteen years of empire resulted from the close connection which had been established between herself and Media. Cyaxares, as already remarked, proceeded from the capture of Nineveh to a long series of wars and conquests. In some, if not in all, of these he appears to have been assisted by the Babylonians, who were perhaps bound by treaty to furnish a contingent as often as he required it, Either Nabopolassar himself, or his son Nebuchadnezzar, would lead out the troops on such occasions; and thus the military spirit of both prince and people would be pretty constantly exercised.

It was as the leader of such a contingent that Nabopolassar was able on one occasion to play the important part of peacemaker in one of the bloodiest of all Cyaxares' wars. After five years' desperate fighting the Medes and Lydians were once more engaged in conflict when an eclipse of the sun took place. Filled with superstitious dread the two armies ceased to contend, and showed a disposition for reconciliation, of which the Babylonian monarch was not slow to take advantage. Having consulted with Syennesis of Cilicia, the foremost man of the allies on the other side, and found him well disposed to second his efforts, he proposed that the sword should be returned to the scabbard, and that a conference should be held to arrange terms of peace. This timely interference proved effectual. A peace was concluded between the Lydians and the Medes, which was cemented by a royal intermarriage: and the result was to give to Western Asia, where war and ravage had long been almost perpetual, nearly half a century of tranquillity.

Successful in his mediation, almost beyond his hopes, Nabopolassar returned from Asia Minor to Babylon. He was now advanced in years, and would no doubt gladly have spent the remainder of his days in the enjoyment of that repose which is so dear to those who feel the infirmities of age creeping upon them. But Providence had ordained otherwise. In B.C. 610—probably the very year of the eclipse-Psammetichus died, and was succeeded by his son Neco, who was in the prime of life and who in disposition was bold and enterprising. This monarch very shortly after his accession cast a covetous eye upon Syria, and in the year B.C. 608, having made vast preparations, he crossed his frontier and invaded the territories of Nabopolassar. Marching along the usual route, by the *Shephilah* and the plain of Esdraelon, he learned, when he neared Megiddo, that a body of troops was drawn up at that place to oppose him, Josiah, the Jewish king, regarding himself as bound to resist the passage through his territories of an army hostile to the monarch of whom he held his crown, had collected his forces, and, having placed them across the line of the invader's march, was calmly awaiting in this position the approach of his master's enemy. Neco hereupon sent ambassadors to persuade Josiah to let him pass, representing that he had no quarrel with the Jews, and claiming a divine sanction to his undertaking. But nothing could shake the Jewish monarch's sense of duty; and Neco was consequently forced to engage with him, and to drive his troops from their position. Josiah, defeated and mortally wounded, returned to Jerusalem, where he died. Neco pressed forward through Syria to the Euphrates; and carrying all before him, established his dominion over the whole tract lying between Egypt on the one hand, and the "Great River" upon the other. On his return three months later he visited Jerusalem, deposed Jehoahaz, a younger son of Josiah, whom the people had made king, and gave the crown to Jehoiakim, his elder brother. It was probably about this time that he besieged and took Gaza, the most important of the Philistine towns next to Ashdod.

The loss of this large and valuable territory did not at once arouse the Babylonian monarch from his inaction or induce him to make any effort for its recovery. Neco enjoyed his conquests in quiet for the space of at least three full years. At length, in the year B.C. 605, Nabopolassar, who felt himself unequal to the fatigues of a campaign, resolved to entrust his forces to Nebuchadnezzar, his son, and to send him to contend with the Egyptians. The key of Syria at this time was Carchemish, a city situated on the right bank of the Euphrates, probably near the site which was afterwards occupied by Hierapolis. Here the forces of Neco were drawn up to protect his conquests, and here Nebuchadnezzar proceeded boldly to attack them. A great battle was fought in the vicinity of the river, which was utterly disastrous to the Egyptians, who "fled away" in confusion, and seem not to have ventured on making a second stand. Nebuchadnezzar rapidly recovered the lost territory, received the submission of Jehoiakim, king of Judah, restored the old frontier line, and probably pressed on into Egypt itself, hoping to cripple or even to crush his presumptuous adversary. But at this point he was compelled to pause. News arrived from Babylon that Nabopolassar was dead; and the Babylonian prince, who feared a disputed succession, having first concluded a hasty arrangement with Neco, returned at his best speed to his capital.

Arriving probably before he was expected, he discovered that his fears were groundless. The priests had taken the direction of affairs during his absence, and the throne had been kept vacant for him by the Chief Priest, or Head of the Order. No pretender had started up to dispute his claims. Doubtless his military prestige, and the probability that the soldiers would adopt his cause, had helped to keep back aspirants; but perhaps it was the promptness of his return, as much as anything, that caused the crisis to pass off without difficulty.

Nebuchadnezzar is the great monarch of the Babylonian Empire, which, lasting only 88 years-from B.C. 625 to B.C. 538—was for nearly half the time under his sway. Its military glory is due chiefly to him, while the constructive energy, which constitutes its especial characteristic, belongs to it still more markedly through his character and genius. It is scarcely too much to say that, but for Nebuchadnezzar, the Babylonians would have had no place in history. At any rate, their actual place is owing almost entirely to this prince, who to the military talents of an able general added a grandeur of artistic conception and a skill in construction which place him on a par with the greatest builders of antiquity.

We have no complete, or even general account of Nebuchadnezzar's wars. Our chief, our almost sole, information concerning them is derived from the Jewish writers. Consequently, those wars only which interested these writers, in other words those whose scene is Palestine or its immediate vicinity, admit of being placed before the reader. If Nebuchadnezzar had quarrels with the Persians, or the Arabians, or the Medes, or the tribes in Mount Zagros, as is not improbable, nothing is now known of their course or issue. Until some historical document belonging to his time shall be discovered, we must be content with a very partial knowledge of the external history of Babylon during his reign. We have a tolerably full account of his campaigns against the Jews, and some information as to the general course of the wars which he carried on with Egypt and Phoenicia; but beyond these narrow limits we know nothing.

It appears to have been only a few years after Nebuchadnezzar's triumphant campaign against Neco that renewed troubles broke out in Syria. Phoenicia revolted under the leadership of Tyre; and about the same time Jehoiakim, the Jewish king, having obtained a promise of aid from the Egyptians, renounced his allegiance. Upon this, in his seventh year (B.C. 598), Nebuchadnezzar proceeded once more into Palestine at the head of a vast army, composed partly of his allies, the Medes, partly of his own subjects. He first invested Tyre; but, finding that city too strong to be taken by assault, he left a portion of his army to continue the siege, while he himself pressed forward against Jerusalem. On his near approach, Jehoiakim, seeing that the Egyptians did not care to come to his aid, made his submission; but Nebuchadnezzar punished his rebellion with death, and, departing from the common Oriental practice, had his dead body treated with indignity. At first he placed upon the throne Jehoia-chin, the son of the late monarch, a youth of eighteen; but three months later, becoming suspicious (probably not without reason) of this prince's fidelity, he deposed him and had him brought a captive to Babylon, substituting in his place his uncle, Zedekiah, a brother of Jehoiakim and Jehoahaz. Meanwhile the siege of Tyre was pressed, but with little effect. A blockade is always tedious; and the blockade of an island city, strong in its navy, by an enemy unaccustomed to the sea, and therefore forced to depend mainly upon the assistance of reluctant allies, must have been a task of such extreme difficulty that one is surprised it was not given up in despair. According to the Tyrian historians their city resisted all the power of Nebuchadnezzar for thirteen years. If this statement is to be relied on, Tyre must have been still uncaptured, when the time came for its sister capital to make that last effort for freedom in which it perished.

After receiving his crown from Nebuchadnezzar, Zedekiah continued for eight years to play the part of a faithful vassal. At length, however, in the ninth year, he fancied he saw a way to independence. A young and enterprising monarch, Uaphris-the Apries of Herodotus-had recently mounted the Egyptian throne. If the alliance of this prince could be secured, there was, Zedekiah thought, a reasonable hope that the yoke of Babylon might be thrown off and Hebrew autonomy re-established. The infatuated monarch did not see that, do what he would, his country had no more than a choice of masters, that by the laws of political attraction Judaea must gravitate to one or other of the two great states between which it had the misfortune of lying. Hoping to free his country, he sent ambassadors to Uaphris, who were to conclude a treaty and demand the assistance of a powerful contingent, composed of both foot and horse. Uaphris received the overture favorably; and Zedekiah at once revolted from Babylon, and made preparations to defend himself with vigor. It was not long before the Babylonians arrived. Determined to crush the daring state, which, weak as it was, had yet ventured to revolt against him now for the fourth time, Nebuchadnezzar came in person, "he and all his host," against Jerusalem, and after overcoming and pillaging the open country, "built forts" and besieged the city. Uaphris, upon this, learning the danger of his ally, marched out of Egypt to his relief; and the Babylonian army, receiving intelligence of his approach, raised the siege and proceeded in quest of their new enemy. According to Josephus a battle was fought, in which the Egyptians were defeated; but it is perhaps more probable that they avoided an engagement by a precipitate retreat into their own country. At any rate the attempt effectually to relieve Jerusalem failed. After a brief interval the siege was renewed; a complete blockade was established; and in a year and a half from the time of the second investment, the city fell.

Nebuchadnezzar had not waited to witness this success of his arms. The siege of Tyre was still being pressed at the date of the second investment of Jerusalem, and the Chaldaean monarch had perhaps thought that his presence on the borders of Phoenicia was necessary to animate his troops in that quarter. If this was his motive in withdrawing from the Jewish capital, the event would seem to have shown that he judged wisely. Tyre, if it fell at the end of its thirteen years' siege, must have been taken in the very year which followed the capture of Jerusalem, B.C. 585. We may suppose that Nebuchadnezzar, when he quitted Jerusalem and took up his abode at Eiblah in the Coele-Syrian valley, turned his main attention to the great Phoenician city, and made arrangements which caused its capture in the ensuing year.

The recovery of these two important cities secured to the Babylonian monarch the quiet possession thenceforth of Syria and Palestine. But still he had not as yet inflicted any chastisement upon Egypt; though policy, no less than honor, required that the aggressions of this audacious power should be punished. If we may believe Josephus, however, the day of vengeance was not very long delayed. Within four years of the fall of Tyre, B.C. 581, Nebuchadnezzar, he tells us, invaded Egypt, put Uaphris, the monarch who had succored Zedekiah, to death, and placed a creature of his own upon the throne. Egyptian history, it is true, forbids our accepting this statement as correct in all its particulars. Uaphris appears certainly to have reigned at least as late as B.C. 569, and according to Herodotus, he was put to death, not by a foreign invader, but by a rebellious subject. Perhaps we may best harmonize the conflicting statements on the subject by supposing that Josephus has confounded two distinct invasions of Egypt, one made by Nebuchadnezzar in his twenty-third year, B.C. 581, which had no very important consequences, and the other eleven years later, B.C. 570, which terminated in the deposition of Uaphris, and the establishment on the throne of a new king, Amasis, who received a nominal royalty from Chaldaean monarch.

Such-as far as they are known-were the military exploits of this great king. He defeated Neco, recovered Syria, crushed rebellion in Judaea, took Tyre, and humiliated Egypt. According to some writers his successes did not stop here. Megasthenes made him subdue most of Africa, and thence pass over into Spain and conquer the Iberians. He even went further, and declared that, on his return from these regions, he settled his Iberian captives on the shores of the Euxine in the country between Armenia and the Caucasus! Thus Nebuchadnezzar was made to reign over an empire extending from the Atlantic to the Caspian, and from the Caucasus to the Great Sahara.

The victories of Nebuchadnezzar were not without an effect on his home administration and on the construction of the vast works with which his name is inseparably associated. It was through them that he obtained that enormous command of "naked human strength" which enabled him, without undue oppression of his own people, to carry out on the grandest scale his schemes for at once beautifying and benefiting his kingdom. From the time when he first took the field at the head of an army he adopted the Assyrian system of forcibly removing almost the whole population of a conquered country, and planting it in a distant part of his dominions. Crowds of captives-the produce of his various wars-Jews, Egyptians, Phoenicians, Syrians, Ammonites, Moabites, were settled in various parts of Mesopotamia, more especially about Babylon. From these unfortunates forced labor was as a matter of course required; and it seems to have been chiefly, if not solely, by their exertions that the magnificent series of great works was accomplished, which formed the special glory of the Fourth Monarchy.

The chief works expressly ascribed to Nebuchadnezzar by the ancient writers are the following: He built the great wall of Babylon, which, according to the lowest estimate, must have contained more than 500,000,000 square feet of solid masonry, and must have required three or four times that number of bricks. He constructed a new and magnificent palace in the neighborhood of the ancient residence of the kings. He made the celebrated "Hanging Garden" for the gratification of his wife, Amyitis. He repaired and beautified the great temple of Belus at Babylon. He dug the huge reservoir near Sippara, said to have been 140 miles in circumference, and 180 feet deep, furnishing it with flood-gates, through which its water could be drawn off for purposes of irrigation. He constructed a number of canals, among them the Nahr Malcha or "Royal River," a broad and deep channel which connected the Euphrates with the Tigris. He built quays and breakwaters along the shores of the Persian Gulf, and he at the same time founded the city of Diridotis or Teredon in the vicinity of that sea.

To these constructions may be added, on the authority either of Nebuchadnezzar's own inscriptions or of the existing remains, the Birs-i-Nimrud, or great temple of Nebo at Bor-sippa; a vast reservoir in Babylon itself, called the Yapur-Shapu; an extensive embankment along the course of the Tigris, near Baghdad; and almost innumerable temples, walls, and other public buildings at Cutha, Sippara, Borsippa, Babylon, Chilmad, Bit-Digla, etc. The indefatigable monarch seems to have either rebuilt, or at least repaired, almost every city and temple throughout the entire country. There are said to be at least a hundred sites in the tract immediately about Babylon, which give evidence, by inscribed bricks bearing his legend, of the marvellous activity and energy of this king.

We may suspect that among the constructions of Nebuchadnezzar was another great work, a work second in utility to none of those above mentioned, and requiring for its completion an enormous amount of labor. This is the canal called by the Arabs the *Kerek Saideh*, or canal of Saideh, which they ascribe to a wife of Nebuchadnezzar, a cutting 400 miles in length, which commenced at Hit on the Euphrates, and was carried along the extreme western edge of the alluvium close to the Arabian frontier, finally falling into the sea at the head of the Bubian creek, about twenty miles to the west of the Shat el-Arab. The traces of this canal which still remain indicate a work of such magnitude and difficulty that we can scarcely ascribe it with probability to any monarch who has held the country since Nebuchadnezzar.

The Pallacopas, or canal of Opa (Palga Opa), which left the Euphrates at Sippara (Mosaib) and ran into a great lake in the neighborhood of Borsippa, whence the lands in the neighborhood were irrigated, may also have been one of Nebuchadnezzar's constructions. It was an old canal, much out of repair, in the time of Alexander, and was certainly the work, not of the Persian conquerors, but of some native monarch anterior to Cyrus. The Arabs, who call it the Nahr Abba, regard it as the oldest canal in the country.

Some glimpses into the private life and personal character of Nebuchadnezzar are afforded us by certain of the Old Testament writers. We see him in the Book of Daniel at the head of a magnificent Court, surrounded by "princes, governors, and captains, judges, treasurers, councillors, and sheriffs;" waited on by eunuchs selected with the greatest care, "well-favored" and carefully educated; attended, whenever he requires it, by a multitude of astrologers and other "wise men," who seek to interpret to him the will of Heaven. He is an absolute monarch, disposing with a word of the lives and properties of his subjects, even the highest. All offices are in his gift. He can raise a foreigner to the second place in the kingdom, and even set him over the entire priestly order. His wealth is enormous, for he makes of pure gold an image, or obelisk, ninety feet high and nine feet broad. He is religious after a sort, but wavers in his faith, sometimes acknowledging the God of the Jews as the only real deity, sometimes relapsing into an idolatrous worship, and forcing all his subjects to follow his example. Even then, however, his polytheism is of a kind which admits of a special devotion to a particular deity, who is called emphatically "his god." In temper he is hasty and violent, but not obstinate; his fierce resolves are taken suddenly and as suddenly repented of; he is moreover capable of bursts of gratitude and devotion, no less than of accesses of fury; like most Orientals, he is vainglorious but he can humble himself before the chastening hand of the Almighty; in his better moods he shows a spirit astonishing in one of his country and time — a spirit of real piety, self-condemnation, and self-abasement, which renders him one of the most remarkable characters in Scripture.

A few touches of a darker hue must be added to this portrait of the great Babylonian king from the statements of another contemporary, the prophet Jeremiah. The execution of Jehoi-akim, and the putting out of Zedekiah's eyes, though acts of considerable severity, may perhaps be regarded as justified by the general practice of the age, and therefore as not indicating in Nebuchadnezzar any special ferocity of disposition. But the ill-treatment of Jehoiakim's dead body, the barbarity of murdering Zedekiah's sons before his eyes, and the prolonged imprisonment both of Zedekiah and of Jehoiachin, though the latter had only contemplated rebellion, cannot be thus excused. They were unusual and unnecessary acts, which tell against the monarch who authorized them, and must be considered to imply a real cruelty of disposition, such as is observable in Sargon and Asshur-bani-pal. Nebuchadnezzar, it is plain, was not content with such a measure of severity as was needed to secure his own interests, but took a pleasure in the wanton infliction of suffering on those who had provoked his resentment.

On the other hand, we obtain from the native writer, Berosus, one amiable trait which deserves a cursory mention. Nebuchadnezzar was fondly attached to the Median princess who had been chosen for him as a wife by his father from political motives. Not content with ordinary tokens of affection, he erected, solely for her gratification, the remarkable structure which the Greeks called the "Hanging Garden." A native of a mountainous country, Amyitis disliked the tiresome uniformity of the level alluvium, and pined for the woods and hills of Media. It was to satisfy this longing by the best substitute which circumstances allowed that the celebrated Garden was made. Art strove to emulate nature with a certain measure of success, and the lofty rocks and various trees of this wonderful Paradise, if they were not a very close imitation of Median mountain scenery, were at any rate a pleasant change from the natural monotony of the Babylonian plain, and must have formed a grateful retreat for the Babylonian queen, whom they reminded at once of her husband's love and of the beauty of her native country.

The most remarkable circumstance in Nebuchadnezzar's life remains to be noticed. Towards the close of his reign, when his conquests and probably most of his great works were completed, in the midst of complete tranquillity and prosperity, a sudden warning was sent him. He dreamt a strange dream, and when he sought to know its meaning, the Prophet Daniel was inspired to tell him that it portended his removal from the kingly office for the space of seven years, in consequence of a curious and very unusual kind of madness. This malady, which is not unknown to physicians, has been termed "Lycanthropy." It consists in the belief that one is not a man but a beast, in the disuse of language, the rejection of all ordinary human food, and sometimes in the loss of the erect posture and a preference for walking on all fours. Within a year of the time that he received the warning, Nebuchadnezzar was smitten. The great king became a wretched maniac. Allowed to indulge in his distempered fancy, he eschewed human habitations, lived in the open air night and day, fed on herbs, disused clothing, and became covered with a rough coat of hair. His subjects generally, it is probable, were not allowed to know of his condition, although they could not but be aware that he was suffering from some terrible malady. The queen most likely held the reins of power, and carried on the government in his name. The dream had been interpreted to mean that the lycanthropy would not be permanent; and even the date of recovery had been announced, only with a certain ambiguity. The Babylonians were thereby encouraged to await events, without taking any steps that would have involved them in difficulties if the malady ceased. And their faith and patience met with a reward. After suffering obscuration for the space of seven years, suddenly the king's intellect returned to him. His recovery was received with joy by his Court. Lords and councillors gathered about him. He once more took the government into his own hands, issued his proclamations, and performed the other functions of royalty. He was now an old man, and his reign does not seem to have been much prolonged; but "the glory of his kingdon," his "honor and brightness" returned; his last days were as brilliant as his first: his sun set in an unclouded sky, shorn of none of the rays that had given splendor to its noonday. Nebuchadnezzar expired at Babylon in the forty-fourth year of his reign, B.C. 561, after an illness of no long duration. He was probably little short of eighty years old at his death.

The successor of Nebuchadnezzar was his son Evil-Mero-dach, who reigned only two years, and of whom very little is known. We may expect that the marvellous events of his father's life, which are recorded in the Book of Daniel, had made a deep impression upon him, and that he was thence inclined to favor the persons, and perhaps the religion, of the Jews. One of his first acts was to release the unfortunate Jehoiachin from the imprisonment in which he had languished for thirty-five years, and to treat him with kindness and respect. He not only recognized his royal rank, but gave him precedence over all the captive kings resident at Babylon. Josephus says that he even admitted Jehoiachin into the number of his most intimate friends. Perhaps he may have designed him some further advancement, and may in other respects have entertained projects which seemed strange and alarming to his subjects. At any rate he had been but two years upon the throne when a conspiracy was formed against him; he was accused of lawlessness and intemperance; his own brother-in-law, Neriglissar, the husband of a daughter of Nebuchadnezzar, headed the malcontents; and Evil-Merodach lost his life with his crown.

Neriglissar, the successful conspirator, was at once acknowledged king. He is probably identical with the "Nergal-shar-ezer, Rab-Mag," of Jeremiah, who occupied a prominent position among the Babylonian nobles left to press the siege of Jerusalem when Nebuchadnezzar retired to Riblah. The title of "Rab-Mag," is one that he bears upon his bricks. It is doubtful what exactly his office was; for we have no reason to believe that there were at this time any Magi at Babylon; but it was certainly an ancient and very high dignity of which even kings might be proud. It is remarkable that Neriglissar calls himself the son of Bel-sum-iskun, "king of Babylon"—a monarch whose name does not appear in Ptolemy's list, but who is probably to be identified with a chieftain so called, who assumed the royal title in the troubles which preceded the fall of the Assyrian Empire.

During his short reign of four years, or rather three years and a few months, Neriglissar had not time to distinguish himself by many exploits. So far as appears, he was at peace with all his neighbors, and employed his time principally in the construction of the Western Palace at Babylon, which was a large building placed at one corner of a fortified inclosure, directly opposite the ancient royal residence, and abutting on the Euphrates. If the account which Diodorus gives of this palace be not a gross exaggeration of the truth, it must have been a magnificent erection, elaborately ornamented with painting and sculpture in the best style of Babylonian art, though in size it may have been inferior to the old residence of the kings on the other side of the river.

Neriglissar reigned from B.C. 559 to B.C. 556, and dying a natural death in the last-named year, left his throne to his son, Laborosoarchod, or Labossoracus. This prince, who was a mere boy, and therefore quite unequal to the task of governing a great empire in critical times, was not allowed to retain the crown many months. Accused by those about him-whether justly or unjustly we cannot say-of giving many indications of a bad disposition, he was deposed and put to death by torture. With him power passed from the House of Nabopolassar, which had held the throne for just seventy years.

On the death of Laborosoarchod the conspirators selected one of their number, a certain Nabonadius or Nabannidochus, and invested him with the sovereignty. He was in no way related to the late monarch, and his claim to succeed must have been derived mainly from the part which he had played in the conspiracy. But still he was a personage of some rank, for his father had, like Neriglissar, held the important office of Rab Mag. It is probable that one of his first steps on ascending the throne was to connect himself by marriage with the royal house which had preceded him in the kingdom. Either the mother of the late king Laborosoarchod, and widow of Neriglissar, or possibly some other daughter of Nebuchadnezzar, was found willing to unite her fortune with those of the new sovereign, and share the dangers and the dignity of his position. Such a union strengthened the hold of the reigning monarch on the allegiance of his subjects, and tended still more to add stability to his dynasty. For as the issue of such a marriage would join in one the claims of both royal houses, he would be sure to receive the support of all parties in the state. Very shortly after the accession of Nabonadius (B.C. 555) he received an embassy from the far north-west. An important revolution had occurred on the eastern frontier of Babylonia three years before, in the reign of Neriglissar; but its effects only now began to make themselves felt among the neighboring nations. Had Cyrus, on taking the crown, adopted the policy of Astyages, the substitution of Persia for Media as the ruling Arian nation would have been a matter of small account. But there can be little doubt that he really entered at once on a career of conquest, Lydia, at any rate, felt herself menaced by the new power, and seeing the danger which threatened the other monarchies of the time, if they allowed the great Arian kingdom to attack them severally with her full force, proposed a league whereby the common enemy might, she thought, be resisted with success. Ambassadors seem to have been sent from Sardis to Babylon in the very year in which Nabonadius became king. He therefore had at once to decide whether he would embrace the offer made him, and uniting with Lydia and Egypt in a league against Persia, make that power his enemy, or refuse the proffered alliance and trust to the gratitude of Cyrus for the future security of his kingdom. It would be easy to imagine the arguments pro and contra which presented themselves to his mind at this conjuncture; but as they would be destitute of a historical foundation, it is perhaps best to state simply the decision at which he is known to have arrived. This was an acceptance of the Lydian offer. Nabonadius consented to join the proposed league; and a treaty was probably soon afterwards concluded between the three powers whereby they united in an alliance offensive and defensive against the Persians.

Knowing that he had provoked a powerful enemy by this bold act, and ignorant how soon he might be called upon to defend his kingdom, from the entire force of his foe, which might be suddenly hurled against him almost at any moment, Nabonadius seems to have turned his attention at once to providing means of defence. The works ascribed by Herodotus to a queen, Nitocris, whom he makes the mother of Nabonadius (Labynetus) must be regarded as in reality constructions of that monarch himself, undertaken with the object of protecting Babylon from Cyrus. They consisted in part of defences within the city, designed apparently to secure it against an enemy who should enter by the river, in part of hydraulic works intended to obstruct the advances of an army by the usual route. The river had hitherto flowed in its natural bed through the middle of the town. Nabonadius confined the stream by a brick embankment carried the whole way along both banks, after which he built on the top of the embankment a wall of a considerable height, pierced at intervals by gateways, in which were set gates of bronze. He likewise made certain cuttings, reservoirs, and sluices at some distance from Babylon towards the north, which were to be hindrances to an enemy's march, though in what way is not very apparent. Some have supposed that besides these works there was further built at the same time a great wall which extended entirely across the tract between the two rivers—a huge barrier a hundred feet high and twenty thick-meant, like the Roman walls in Britain and the great wall of China, to be insurmountable by an unskillful foe; but there is ground for suspecting that this belief is ill-founded, having for its sole basis a misconception of Xenophon's.

Nabonadius appears to have been allowed ample time to carry out to the full his system of defences, and to complete all his preparations. The precipitancy of Croesus, who plunged into a war with Persia single-handed, asking no aid from his allies, and the promptitude of Cyrus, who allowed him no opportunity of recovering from his first false step, had prevented Nabonadius from coming into actual collision with Persia in the early part of his reign. The defeat of Croesus in the battle of Pteria, the siege of Sardis, and its capture, followed so rapidly on the first commencement of hostilities, that whatever his wishes may have been, Nabonadius had it not in his power to give any help to his rash ally. Actual war was thus avoided at this time; and no collision having occurred, Cyrus could defer an attack on the great kingdom of the south until he had consolidated his power in the north and the northeast, which he rightly regarded as of the last importance. Thus fourteen years intervened between the capture of Sardis by the Persian arms and the commencement of the expedition against Babylon.

When at last it was rumored that the Persian king had quitted Ecbatana (B.C. 539) and commenced his march to the south-west, Nabonadius received the tidings with indifference. His defences were completed: his city was amply provisioned; if the enemy should defeat him in the open field, he might retire behind his walls, and laugh to scorn all attempts to reduce his capital either by blockade or storm. It does not appear to have occurred to him that it was possible to protect his territory. With a broad, deep, and rapid river directly interposed between him and his foe, with a network of canals spread far and wide over his country, with an almost inexhaustible supply of human labor at his command for the construction of such dikes, walls, or cuttings as he should deem advisable, Nabonadius might, one would have thought, have aspired to save his land from invasion, or have disputed inch by inch his enemy's advance towards the capital. But such considerations have seldom had much force with Orientals, whose notions of war and strategy are even now of the rudest and most primitive description. To measure one's strength as quickly as possible with that of one's foe, to fight one great pitched battle in order to decide the question of superiority in the field, and then, if defeated, either to surrender or to retire behind walls, has been the ordinary conception of a commander's duties in the East from the time of the Ramesside kings to our own day. No special blame therefore attaches to Nabonadius for his neglect. He followed the traditional policy of Oriental monarchs in the course which he took. And his subjects had less reason to complain of his resolution than most others, since the many strongholds in Babylonia must have afforded them a ready refuge, and the great fortified district within which Babylon itself stood must have been capable of accommodating with ease the whole native population of the country.

If we may trust Herodotus, the invader, having made all his preparations and commenced his march, came to a sudden pause midway between Ecbatana and Babylon. One of the sacred white horses, which drew the chariot of Ormazd, had been drowned in crossing a river; and Cyrus had thereupon desisted from his march, and, declaring that he would revenge himself on the insolent stream, had set his soldiers to disperse its waters into 360 channels. This work employed him during the whole summer and autumn; nor was it till another spring had come that he resumed his expedition. To the Babylonians such a pause must have appeared like irresolution. They must have suspected that the invader had changed his mind and would not venture across the Tigris. If the particulars of the story reached them, they probably laughed at the monarch who vented his rage on inanimate nature, while he let his enemies escape scot free.

Cyrus, however, had a motive for his proceedings which will appear in the sequel. Having wintered on the banks of the Gyndes in a mild climate, where tents would have been quite a sufficient protection to his army, he put his troops in motion at the commencement of spring, crossed the Tigris apparently unopposed, and soon came in sight of the capital. Here he found the Babylonian army drawn out to meet him under the command of Nabonadius himself, who had resolved to try the chance of a battle. An engagement ensued, of which we possess no details; our informants simply tell us that the Babylonian monarch was completely defeated, and that, while most of his army sought safety within the walls of the capital, he himself with a small body of troops threw himself into Borsippa, an important town lying at a short distance from Babylon towards the south-west. It is not easy to see the exact object of this movement. Perhaps Nabonadius thought that the enemy would thereby be obliged to divide his army, which might then more easily be defeated; perhaps he imagined that by remaining without the walls he might be able to collect such a force among his subjects and allies as would compel the beleaguering army to withdraw. Or, possibly, he merely followed an instinct of self-preservation, and fearing that the soldiers of Cyrus might enter Babylon with his own, if he fled thither, sought refuge in another city.

It might have been supposed that his absence would have produced anarchy and confusion in the capital; but a step which he had recently taken with the object of giving stability to his throne rendered the preservation of order tolerably easy. At the earliest possible moment- probably when he was about fourteen-he had associated with him in the government his son, Belshazzar, or Bel-shar-uzur, the grandson of the great Nebuchadnezzar. This step, taken most likely with a view to none but internal dangers, was now found exceedingly convenient for the purposes of the war. In his father's absence Belshazzar took the direction of affairs within the city, and met and foiled for a considerable time all the assaults of the Persians. He was young and inexperienced, but he had the counsels of the queen-mother to guide and support him, as well as those of the various lords and officers of the court. So well did he manage the defence that after a while Cyrus despaired, and as a last resource ventured on a stratagem in which it was clear that he must either succeed or perish.

Withdrawing the greater part of his army from the vicinity of the city, and leaving behind him only certain corps of observation, Cyrus marched away up the course of the Euphrates for a certain distance, and there proceeded to make a vigorous use of the spade. His soldiers could now appreciate the value of the experience which they had gained by dispersing the Gyndes, and perceive that the summer and autumn of the preceding year had not been wasted. They dug a channel or channels from the Euphrates, by means of which a great portion of its water would be drawn off, and hoped in this way to render the natural course of the river fordable.

When all was prepared, Cyrus determined to wait for the arrival of a certain festival, during which the whole population were wont to engage in drinking and revelling, and then silently in the dead of night to turn the water of the river and make his attack. It fell out as he hoped and wished. The festival was held with even greater pomp and splendor than usual; for Belshazzar, with the natural insolence of youth, to mark his contempt of the besieging army, abandoned himself wholly to the delights of the season, and himself entertained a thousand lords in his palace. Elsewhere the rest of the population was occupied in feasting and dancing. Drunken riot and mad excitement held possession of the town; the siege was forgotten; ordinary precautions were neglected. Following the example of their king, the Babylonians gave themselves up for the night to orgies in which religious frenzy and drunken excess formed a strange and revolting medley.

Meanwhile, outside the city, in silence and darkness, the Persians watched at the two points where the Euphrates entered and left the walls. Anxiously they noted the gradual sinking of the water in the river-bed; still more anxiously they watched to see if those within the walls would observe the suspicious circumstance and sound an alarm through the town. Should such an alarm be given, all their labors would be lost. If, when they entered the river-bed, they found the river-walls manned and the river-gates fast-locked, they would be indeed "caught in a trap." Enfiladed on both sides by an enemy whom they could neither see nor reach, they would be overwhelmed and destroyed by his missiles before they could succeed in making their escape. But, as they watched, no sounds of alarm reached them-only a confused noise of revel and riot, which showed that the unhappy townsmen were quite unconscious of the approach of danger.

At last shadowy forms began to emerge from the obscurity of the deep river-bed, and on the landing-places opposite the river-gates scattered clusters of men grew into solid columns-the undefended gateways were seized —a war-shout was raised-the alarm was taken and spread-and swift runners started off to "show the King of Babylon that his city was taken at one end." In the darkness and confusion of the night a terrible massacre ensued. The drunken revellers could make no resistance. The king paralyzed with fear at the awful handwriting upon the wall, which too late had warned him of his peril, could do nothing even to check the progress of the assailants, who carried all before them everywhere. Bursting into the palace, a band of Persians made their way to the presence of the monarch, and slew him on the scene of his impious revelry. Other bands carried fire and sword through the town. When morning came, Cyrus found himself undisputed master of the city, which, if it had not despised his efforts, might with the greatest ease have baffled them.

The war, however, was not even yet at an end. Nabonadius still held Borsippa, and, if allowed to remain unmolested, might have gradually gathered strength and become once more a formidable foe. Cyrus, therefore, having first issued his orders that the outer fortifications of Babylon should be dismantled, proceeded to complete his conquest by laying siege to the town where he knew that Nabonadius had taken refuge. That monarch, however, perceiving that resistance would be vain, did not wait till Borsippa was invested, but on the approach of his enemy surrendered himself. Cyrus rewarded his submission by kind and liberal treatment. Not only did he spare his life, but (if we may trust Abydenus) he conferred on him the government of the important province of Carmania.

Thus perished the Babylonian empire. If we seek the causes of its fall, we shall find them partly in its essential military inferiority to the kingdom that had recently grown up upon its borders, partly in the accidental circumstance that its ruler at the time of the Persian attack was a man of no great capacity. Had Nebuchadnezzar himself, or a prince of his mental calibre, been the contemporary of Cyrus, the issue of the contest might have been doubtful. Babylonia possessed naturally vast powers of resistance-powers which, had they been made use of to the utmost, might have tired out the patience of the Persians. That lively, active, but not over-persevering people would scarcely have maintained a siege with the pertinacity of the Babylonians themselves or of the Egyptians. If the stratagem of Cyrus had failed-and its success depended wholly on the Babylonians exercising no vigilance-the capture of the town would have been almost impossible. Babylon was too large to be blockaded; its walls were too lofty to be scaled, and too massive to be battered down by the means possessed by the ancients. Mining in the soft alluvial soil would have been dangerous work, especially as the town ditch was deep and supplied with abundant water from the Euphrates. Cyrus, had he failed in his night attack, would probably have at once raised the siege; and Babylonian independence might perhaps in that case have been maintained down to the time of Alexander.

Even thus, however, the "Empire" would not have been continued. So soon as it became evident that the Babylonians were no match for the Persians in the field, their authority over the subject nations was at an end. The Susianians, the tribes of the middle Euphrates, the Syrians, the Phoenicians, the Jews, the Idumseans, the Ammonites and Moabites, would have gravitated to the stronger power, even if the attack of Cyrus on Babylon itself had been repulsed. For the conquests of Cyrus in Asia Minor, the Oxus region, and Afghanistan, had completely destroyed the balance of power in Western Asia, and given to Persia a preponderance both in men and in resources against which the cleverest and most energetic of Babylonian princes would have struggled in vain. Persia must in any case have absorbed all the tract between Mount Zagros and the Mediterranean, except Babylonia Proper; and thus the successful defence of Babylon would merely have deprived the Persian Empire of a province.

In its general character the Babylonian Empire was little more than a reproduction of the Assyrian. The same loose organization of the provinces under native kings rather than satraps almost universally prevailed, with the same duties on the part of suzerain and subjects and the same results of ever-recurring revolt and re-conquest. Similar means were employed under both empires to check and discourage rebellion-mutilations and executions of chiefs, pillage of the rebellious region, and wholesale deportation of its population. Babylon, equally with Assyria, failed to win the affections of the subject nations, and, as a natural result, received no help from them in her hour of need. Her system was to exhaust and oppress the conquered races for the supposed benefit of the conquerors, and to impoverish the provinces for the adornment and enrichment of the capital. The wisest of her monarch's thought it enough to construct works of public utility in Babylonia Proper, leaving the dependent countries to themselves, and doing nothing to develop their resources. This selfish system was, like most selfishness, short-sighted; it alienated those whom it would have been true policy to conciliate and win. When the time of peril came, the subject nations were no source of strength to the menaced empire, On the contrary, it would seem that some even turned against her and made common cause with the assailants.

Babylonian civilization differed in many respects from Assyrian, to which however it approached more nearly than to any other known type. Its advantages over Assyrian were in its greater originality, its superior literary character, and its comparative width and flexibility. Babylonia seems to have been the source from which Assyria drew her learning, such as it was, her architecture, the main ideas of her mimetic art, her religious notions, her legal forms, and a vast number of her customs and usages. But Babylonia herself, so far as we know, drew her stores from no foreign country. Hers was apparently the genius which excogitated an alphabet-worked out the simpler problems of arithmetic-invented implements for measuring the lapse of time-conceived the idea of raising enormous structures with the poorest of all materials, clay-discovered the art of polishing, boring, and engraving gems-reproduced with truthfulness the outlines of human and animal forms-attained to high perfection in textile fabrics-studied with success the motions of the heavenly bodies-conceived of grammar as a science-elaborated a system of law-saw the value of an exact chronology-in almost every branch of science made a beginning, thus rendering it comparatively easy for other nations to proceed with the superstructure. To Babylonia, far more than to Egypt, we owe the art and learning of the Greeks. It was from the East, not from Egypt, that Greece derived her architecture, her sculpture, her science, her philosophy, her mathematical knowledge-in a word, her intellectual life. And Babylon was the source to which the entire stream of Eastern civilization may be traced. It is scarcely too much to say that, but for Babylon, real civilization might not even yet have dawned upon the earth. Mankind might never have advanced beyond that spurious and false form of it which in Egypt, India, China, Japan, Mexico, and Peru, contented the aspirations of the species.

Appendix.

A. Standard Inscription of Nebuchadnezzar

The Inscription begins with the various titles of Nebuchadnezzar. It then contains prayers and invocations to the Gods, Merodach and Nebo. The extent of N.'s power is spoken of-it reaches from one sea to the other.

An account is then given of the wonders of Babylon, viz.:
1. The great temple of Merodach. (The mound of Babil is the tower or ziggurat of this.)
2. The Borsippa temple (or Birs).
3. Various other temples in Babylon and Borsippa.

The subjoined description of the city follows: "The double inclosure which Nabopolassar my father had made but not completed, I finished. Nabopolassar made its ditch. With two long embankments of brick and mortar he bound its bed. He made the embankment of the Arahha. He lined the other side of the Euphrates with brick. He made a bridge (?) over the Euphrates, but did not finish its buttresses (?). From... (the name of a place) he made with bricks burnt as hard as stones, by the help of the great Lord Merodach, a way (for) a branch of the Shimat to the waters of the Yapur-Shapu, the great reservoir of Babylon, opposite to the gate of Nin.

"The *Ingur-Bel* and the *Nimiti-Bel* —the great double wall of Babylon—I finished. With two long embankments of brick and mortar I built the sides of its ditch. I joined it on with that which my father had made. I strengthened the city. Across the river to the west I built the wall of Babylon with brick. The Yapur-Shapu-the reservoir of Babylon-by the grace of Merodach I filled completely full of water. With bricks burnt as hard as stones, and with bricks in huge masses like mountains (?), the Yapur-Shapu, from the gate of Mula as far as Nana, who is the protectress of her votaries, by the grace of his godship (i.e. Merodach) I strengthened. With that which my father had made I joined it. I made the way of Nana, the protectress of her votaries. The great gates of the Ingur-Bel and the Nimiti-Bel-the reservoir of Babylon, at the time of the flood (lit. of fulness), inundated them. These gates I raised. Against the waters their foundations with brick and mortar I built. [Here follows a description of the gates, with various architectural details, an account of the decorations, hangings, etc.] For the delight of mankind I filled the reservoir. Behold! besides the Ingur-Bel, the impregnable fortification of Babylon. I constructed inside Babylon on the eastern side of the river a fortification such as no king had ever made before me, viz., a long rampart, 4000 ammas square, as an extra defence. I excavated the ditch: with brick and mortar I bound its bed; a long rampart at its head (?) I strongly built. I adorned its gates. The folding doors and the pillars I plated with copper. Against presumptuous enemies, who were hostile to the men of Babylon, great waters, like the waters of the ocean, I made use of abundantly. Their depths were like the depths of the vast ocean. I did not allow the waters to overflow, but the fulness of their floods I caused to flow on, restraining them with a brick embankment.... Thus I completely made strong the defences of Babylon. May it last forever!"

[Here follows a similar account of works at Borsippa.] "In Babylon-the city which is the delight of my eyes, and which I have glorified-when the waters were in flood, they inundated the foundations of the great palace called Taprati-nisi, or 'the Wonder of Mankind;' (a palace) with many chambers and lofty towers; the high-place of Royalty; (situated) in the land of Babylon, and in the middle of Babylon; stretching from the Ingur-Bel to the bed of the Shebil, the eastern canal, (and) from the bank of the Sippara river, to the water of the Yapur-Shapu; which Nabopolassar my father built with brick and raised up; when the reservoir of Babylon was full, the gates of this palace were flooded. I raised the mound of brick on which it was built, and made smooth its platform. I cut off the floods of the water, and the foundations (of the palace) I protected against the water with bricks and mortar: and I finished it completely. Long beams

I set up to support it: with pillars and beams plated with copper and strengthened with iron I built up its gates. Silver and gold, and precious stones whose names were almost unknown [here follow several unknown names of objects, treasures of the palace], I stored up inside, and placed there the treasure-house of my kingdom. Four years (?), the seat of my kingdom in the city..., which....did not rejoice (my) heart. In all my dominions I did not build a high-place of power; the precious treasures of my kingdom I did not lay up. In Babylon, buildings for myself and the honor of my kingdom I did not lay out. In the worship of Merodach my lord, the joy of my heart (?), in Babylon, the city of his sovereignty and the seat of my empire, I did not sing his praises (?), and I did not furnish his altars (i.e. with victims), nor did I clear out the canals." [Here follow further negative clauses.]

"As a further defence in war, at the Ingur-Bel, the impregnable outer wall, the rampart of the Babylonians-with two strong lines of brick and mortar I made a strong fort, 400 ammas square inside the Nimiti-Bel, the inner defence of the Babylonians. Masonry of brick within them (the lines) I constructed. With the palace of my father I connected it. In a happy month and on an auspicious day its foundations I laid in the earth like....I completely finished its top. In fifteen days I completed it, and made it the high-place of my kingdom. [Here follows a description of the ornamentation of the palace.] A strong fort of brick and mortar in strength I constructed. Inside the brick fortification another great fortification of long stones, of the size of great mountains, I made. Like Shedim I raised up its head. And this building I raised for a wonder; for the defence of the people I constructed it."

B. On The Meanings of Babylonian Names

The names of the Babylonians, like those of the Assyrians, were significant. Generally, if not always, they were composed of at least two elements. These might be a noun in the nominative case with a verb following it, a noun in the nominative with a participle in apposition, or a word meaning "servant" followed by the name of a god. Under the first class came such names as "Bel-ipni" —"Bel has made (me)" —from Bel, the name of the God, and hana (Heb. בָּנָה), " to make;" Nabo-nassar—" Nebo protects (me)" —from Nebo and nazar (Heb. נָצַר), " to guard, protect;" and Nebo-sallim —"Nebo makes perfect" —from Nebo and a verb cognate with the Hebrew שָׁלֵם, which in the Piel has the meaning of "complete, make perfect." Names compounded with a noun and participle are such as Nebo-nahid and Nahid-Merodach. Here nahid is the participle active of a verb, nahad, cognate with the Arabic نهد, and the Hebrew הוֹד, meaning "to make prosperous" or "bless." A specimen of a name compounded with a word meaning " servant " and the appellation of a god seems to exist in Abed-nego —more properly Abed-Nebo —from abed (Heb. עֶבֶד), " a slave," and Nebo, the well-known and favourite god.

More usually a Babylonian name consists of three elements, a noun in the nominative, a verb or participle, and a noun in the accusative following the verb. To this class belong the following : —Nabopolassar, Nebuchadnezzar, Neriglissar, Belsliazzar, Merodach-baladan, Merodach-iddin-akhi, Merodachsum-adin, Merodacli-sbapik-ziri, Ncbo-bil-sumi, and Nebuzaradan.

Nabopolassar, or more properly Nabu-pal-uzur, means " Nebo protects (my) son," being formed from the roots *Nabu*, " Nebo," *pal*, "son," and *nazar*, "to protect." Nebuchadnezzar, or Nebuchadrezzar (in the original, Nabu-kudurri- uzur), means either "Nebo is the protector of landmarks," or "Nebo protects the youth." The first and last elements are the same as in Nabopolassar : the middle element *kudur* is a word of very doubtful meaning. It has been connected by some with the Persian κίδαρις, "crown." M. Oppert explains it from the Arabic كَدَر, which means " a young man." Sir H. Kawlinson regards it as meaning "a landmark."

Neriglissar and Belshazzar are names of exactly the same kind. The former, correctly written, is Nergal-sar-uzur ; the latter, Bil-sar-uzur. The one means " Nergal protects the king ;" the other, " Bel protects the king." The only new element here is the middle one, *sar*, " king " (Heb. שַׂר), which is found in Sargon, and perhaps in Shar-ezer.

In Merodach-bal-adan (or Marduk-bal-*iddin*) we have *bal*, a variant of *pal*, "a son," and *iddin*, the 3rd person singular of *nadan*, "to give " (comp. Heb. נָתַן). The name consequently means "Merodach has given a son." Similarly, in Marduk-iddin-akhi we have *iddin* from *nadan*, together with *akhi*, the plural of *akhu*, "a brother ;" and the meaning of the name is thus "Merodach has given brothers." The two roots Merodach and iddin appear also in Merodach-sum-adan (or Marduk-sum-iddin) in conjunction with a new root, sum, "a name" (comp. Heb. שֵׁם); and there results the meaning "Merodach has given a name" —or perhaps "Merodach is the giver of fame;" since the Hebrew שֵׁם has likewise that signification.

Merodach-shapik-ziri may be translated "Merodach produces offspring," the root *shapik* being connected with שָׁפַךְ, "to pour out," derivatives from which have a genitive sense, as שִׁפְכָה and *ziri* being the plural of *zir*, a root meaning "seed, race, offspring" (comp. Heb. זֶרַע).

In Nabu-bil-sumi, *bil* is used in its original sense of "lord" (comp. Heb. בַּעַל), while *sumi* is the plural of sum, "a name." The meaning is thus "Nebo presides over names," or "Nebo is the lord of names."

Nebu-zar-adan is probably a Hebrew corruption of Nebuzir- iddin, which means "Nebo has given offspring," from roots already explained.

The bulk of the Babylonian names preserved to us in Ptolemy's Canon do not admit of any certain explanation, from the corrupt shape in which they have come down to us. Occasionally we may recognise with some confidence the name of a god in them, as Merodach in Meses*imordach*us and Bel in Regi*bel*us ; but attempts to give the full actual etymology can only be the merest conjectures," with which it would not be worth while to trouble the reader. A few probable explanations of some Babylonian names preserved by the Hebrews, and probably very little changed, will alone be attempted before bringing these remarks on Babylonian nomenclature to a conclusion.

The Samgar-Nebo of Jeremiah probably signifies "one who is devoted to Nebo," *Samgar* being a *shaphel* form from the root migir, which means "honouring" or "obeying." Sarsechim, in the same writer, is perhaps "the king consents," from *sar* and the Chaldee סכם, which becomes in the *aphel* אסכים, and has that meaning. Belteshazzar, the name given by the prince of the eunuchs to Daniel, would have appeared, from the obvious analogy of Belshazzar, to be a contracted form of Bilta-shar-uzur, and therefore to signify "Beltis protects the king." But it is an objection to this that Nebuchadnezzar connects the name with that of "his god," who must (it would seem) be Bel, and not Beltis. If then we are obliged to seek another derivation, we may perhaps find it in Bel, the god, *tisha* (Heb. לטישא), "a secret," and *uzur*, from *nazar*, "to guard, protect." Belteshazzar would then mean "Bel is the keeper of secrets," an appropriate sense, since "secrets" were what Daniel was considered especially to know.

It will be observed that almost every Babylonian name, the etymology of which is known to us, has a religious character. Among the elements is almost universally to be recognised the name of a god. The gods especially favoured are Nebo and Merodach, after whom comes Bel, and then Nergal and Shamas. In the kind of religious sentiment which they express the names closely resemble those of the Assyrians." First, there are names announcing facts of the mythology ; as Nebuchadrezzar, "Nebo protects landmarks," Belteshazzar, "Bel guards secrets." Next, there are those in which a glorification of the deity is made, as Nabu-bil-sumi, "Nebo is the lord of names," Nabu-sallim, "Nebo makes perfect," and the like. Thirdly, a number of names contain the idea of thankfulness to the god who has granted the child in answer to prayer, as Merodach-bal-adan, "Merodach has given a son," Bel-ipni, "Bel has made (him)," Nebu-zar-adan, "Nebo has given the offspring," &c. And, finally, there are those which imply special devotion of the individual to a particular deity, either directly, as Shamgar-Nebo, " the devotee of Nebo," Abed-Nebo, " the slave of Nebo," or indirectly, as Nabo-nassar, " Nebo protects (me)," Nabopolassar, "Nebo protects (my) son," Belshazzar, " Bel protects the king," Nabo-nahid, "Nebo (is) protecting (me)," and the like.

In the comparatively rare case of names which contain no divine element, the honour of the king seems to have been sometimes, but not very often, considered. In Yakin, Nadina, Zakiru, Balazu, Hagisa, Arioch, Susub, names which seem to be of a purely secular character, there is contained no flattery of the monarch. Thus far then the Babylonians would appear to have been of a more independent spirit than the Assyrians, with whom this species of adulation was not infrequent.

Printed in Great Britain
by Amazon